HOLLYWOOD
STARS WHO DIED TOO YOUNG

For Jackie, Mary and Amy: gone too soon and missed every day.

HOLLYWOOD STARS WHO DIED TOO YOUNG

KATHERINE BEBO

WHITE OWL
AN IMPRINT OF PEN & SWORD BOOKS LTD.
YORKSHIRE – PHILADELPHIA

First published in Great Britain in 2026 by
PEN AND SWORD WHITE OWL
An imprint of
Pen & Sword Books Ltd
Yorkshire – Philadelphia

Print ISBN 978 1 39900 402 2
ePUB ISBN 978 1 39900 403 9
ePDF ISBN 978 1 39900 405 3

A CIP catalogue record for this book is available from the British Library.

Typeset in Times New Roman 10.5/14 by
SJmagic DESIGN SERVICES, India.
Printed and bound in the UK by CPI Group (UK) Ltd, Croydon CR0 4YY.

The Publisher's authorised representative in the EU for product safety is Authorised Rep Compliance Ltd., Ground Floor, 71 Lower Baggot Street, Dublin D02 P593, Ireland.
www.arccompliance.com

For a complete list of Pen & Sword titles please contact

PEN & SWORD BOOKS LIMITED
George House, Units 12 & 13, Beevor Street, Off Pontefract Road,
Barnsley, South Yorkshire S71 1HN, England
E-mail: enquiries@pen-and-sword.co.uk
Website: www.pen-and-sword.co.uk

or

PEN AND SWORD BOOKS
1950 Lawrence Road, Havertown, PA 19083, USA
E-mail: uspen-and-sword@casematepublishers.com
Website: www.penandswordbooks.com

FSC
www.fsc.org
MIX
Paper | Supporting responsible forestry
FSC® C013604

Contents

INTRODUCTION

The Great Casting Call in the Sky

'They've great respect for the
dead in Hollywood, but
none for the living' – Errol Flynn

Sean Connery was 90 when he died… Gene Hackman was 95… Betty White was 99… While each of these Hollywood stars enjoyed a full and fruitful life, others weren't so lucky. Between the drug overdoses, suicides, accidents, health conditions and murders that resulted in untimely deaths, Tinseltown has seen its fair share of tragedy. Some Hollywood deaths are woeful beyond belief. Take Peg Entwistle. This 1930s actress desperate to be a star only appeared in one film – *Thirteen Women* – before she climbed to the top of the 'H' of the 'HOLLYWOODLAND' (now 'HOLLYWOOD') sign and hurled herself from the top. Had she lived, she could have gone on to dazzle in dozens of Golden Age box-office hits, won a handful of Oscars and made her mark on history as a legendary starlet. We'll never know.

We'll also never know what more Marilyn Monroe, James Dean, Chadwick Boseman or Brittany Murphy could have achieved had their lives not been cut short. But these long-gone legends live on through their movies, in the awestruck audience's memory and, now, in the pages of *Hollywood Stars Who Died Too Young*. Join me as we look back at their lives, their careers, their loves, their losses, their highs, their lows… and the legacies and loved ones they have left behind. Each star in the book achieved a lot during their time on this Earth, blissfully unaware of their fate. They lived for their craft and, in some cases, died as a result of the trappings of fame.

But this is not just a collection of tragedies; it is a celebration of the selected stars' raw talent and a tribute to their trade. Some, like Elvis Presley, had already reached their peak, whereas others, like Sharon Tate, were just getting started, leaving their untapped promise and unrealized potential to linger.

So pop some corn, grab some tissues and prepare to walk down the red carpet with some of your favourite late Hollywood stars, who heard the phrase 'That's a wrap' far too soon.

John Belushi

Age of death: 33

Date of death: 5 March 1982

Cause of death: Drug overdose

'In your twenties, you feel like you're indestructible... In your thirties, you think "I'll be around here a little longer, so I'm going to take better care of myself".'

His Life

If there's something strange in your neighbourhood, who you gonna call? Well, if John Belushi hadn't died, you'd have called him, along with his Ghostbusting buddies Dan Aykroyd, Harold Ramis and Ernie Hudson. As it turned out, Bill Murray played the part that had been written for Belushi, and his old pal Aykroyd joked that the wild Slimer was 'the ghost of John Belushi'. Other roles the zany actor had been cast for but never got to play included Ned Nederlander in *Three Amigos*, which was recast with Martin Short; and Max Bercovicz in *Once Upon a Time in America*, which ultimately went to James Woods. This latter part could have been a turning point in Belushi's career, seeing him in a dramatic role. Prior to this, the only serious film he'd been in was the 1979 *Old Boyfriends*, with his other movies – like *National Lampoon's Animal House, Goin' South, 1941*, *Continental Divide* and *Neighbors* – being comedies.

Comedy was where Chicago-born Belushi shone. Via The Second City comedy enterprise and *The National Lampoon Radio Hour*, in 1975, he began his reign on the new *NBC's Saturday Night* – later to become the still-going-strong *Saturday Night Live* (*SNL*). One of the original seven cast members, for four years he cracked audiences up with his out-there characters, including Beethoven, Henry Kissinger, Captain Kirk, Samurai Fataba, Pete Dionisopoulos and the ranty guy on the Weekend Update sketch who coined the phrase 'But NOOOOOOO!' (which was later parodied by Mouth – Corey Feldman – in the 1985 *The Goonies*). The Blues Brothers were also born on *SNL*, originally created to warm up the studio audience with their musical numbers. Aykroyd and Belushi made their debut as the black-suited, hat-donning, shades-wearing Jake and Elwood on the show on 22 April 1978, with Belushi cartwheeling onto the stage and belting out a rendition of 'Soul Man'. The same year, they released their debut music album *Briefcase Full of Blues*, and in 1979, they quit *SNL* to make *The Blues Brothers* movie. On set, Belushi earned the nickname 'The Black Hole' as he kept losing his sunglasses and is said to have gone through hundreds of pairs.

He also went through masses of cocaine. The film's budget had a dedicated portion for the drug in order to help everyone stay alert during night shoots. There was even an on-set private bar named The Blues Club, where cast, crew and friends could acquire any drug they wanted from the bar staff. Described by Aykroyd as 'a good man but a bad boy', Belushi was at the height of his cocaine addiction whilst filming *The Blues Brothers*, and his partying would often hold up production on the film. Director John Landis (who Belushi had also worked with on *National Lampoon's Animal House*) said of the actor's drug habit: 'It was terrible. He went from being this really sweet guy to someone hyper and maniacal.' The class-A drug had previously done him no favours on the set of *SNL* either – due to his behaviour, he was fired (then rehired) from the show several times. Fellow *SNL* comedian Jane Curtin admitted years later that she'd had issues with John, but acknowledged that, at the time, he wasn't himself; he was an addict. Indeed, John admitted that he liked ruffling feathers, saying, 'I'd rather be an anarchist than a professional.'

Despite being an 'anarchist', the actor, comedian and musician sure did have a lot of professional success. In 1978, he was at the top of his game and one of the biggest stars in Hollywood, with a number-one movie (*National Lampoon's Animal House*, which at the time was the highest-grossing comedy ever), a number-one TV show (*SNL*) and a number-one album (*Briefcase Full of Blues*, which reached number one on the Billboard album chart and went double platinum). The year before, the comic genius had won a Primetime Emmy for his writing on *SNL*. Indeed, it seemed like there was no stopping him. When talking about his comedy style, his wife Judy Jacklin – who had been his high-school sweetheart – remarked: 'He went from zero to 100 so quickly, and that surprised people.'

One particular *SNL* skit titled 'Don't Look Back in Anger', which aired in 1978, has become rather poignant. In it, an elderly John Belushi, complete with white bushy eyebrows and a moustache, is visiting the graves of his *SNL* co-stars. As he's doddering along, he says, 'They all thought I'd be the first to go. I was one of those live-fast, die-young, leave-a-good-looking-corpse types.' He points to each of his friend's graves and outlines how they died. When he gets to Garrett Morris, he explains that he died of an overdose of heroin, which elicits a big laugh from the audience. 'Why me?' Belushi asks. 'Why did I live so long? They're all dead. I'll tell you why. Cuz I'm a dancer.' And he breaks out into a jig.

His Death

Belushi stopped dancing on 5 March 1982, at the age of 33. He was found dead by his fitness trainer in the Chateau Marmont hotel bungalow he had been renting out. The actor had been injected with a mixture of heroin and cocaine – a lethal combination known as a 'speedball'. In the days prior to this, he had been partying hard in the nightclubs on Los Angeles' Sunset Strip and Santa Monica Boulevard, taking plenty of drugs as he went. Fellow Hollywood stars Robert De Niro and Robin Williams had been in Belushi's room the night of his death, but didn't stay long as they were 'creeped out' by the 'trashy' woman who was also there. She turned out to be drug dealer Cathy Smith and was the person who injected Belushi with the speedball after Williams and De Niro had left. Smith later pleaded guilty to involuntary manslaughter and served fifteen months in prison. Following the death of his friend, Williams – who was no stranger to several lines of coke himself – cleaned up his act, saying: 'Here's this guy who's a beast, who could do anything, and he's gone. That sobered the shit out of me.'

Belushi's funeral was held on 9 March in Abel's Hill Cemetery in Chilmark on the island of Martha's Vineyard, Massachusetts. Dan Aykroyd, who had bought a house on Martha's Vineyard at the encouragement of Belushi, was one of the pallbearers, and led the procession from the church to the cemetery on his motorcycle. Graveside, James Taylor sang 'That Lonesome Road'. Belushi's tombstone has a skull and crossbones on, with the inscription: 'I may be gone, but Rock and Roll lives on.' Having earned a reputation as a party animal, fans visiting his grave would often disturb the peace with excess noise, leaving beer cans, liquor bottles and drug paraphernalia, even doing lines of cocaine on the headstone. As such, a little over a year after his funeral, Belushi's family decided to have his body exhumed and reburied in an unmarked grave near the original site. The tombstone of Belushi's mother and father – Agnes and Adam – at Elmwood Cemetery in River Grove, Illinois has John's name inscribed on it, with the words 'In loving memory of our son. He gave us laughter.' It serves as a cenotaph where fans can visit to pay their respects.

The star had been scheduled to present the Best Visual Effects Oscar at the 1982 Academy Awards with Dan Aykroyd. As Aykroyd was undoing the winner's envelope, he quipped: 'My partner, he would have loved presenting this award with me, he was somewhat of a visual effect himself.' Fellow *SNL* comedian Brian Doyle-Murray (Bill Murray's brother) gave a touching tribute to Belushi during the first episode of the show since his death. He regaled the story of when his friend had pushed him out of the way of a ten-tonne truck, only to be hit by it himself. Murray said that Belushi got up, dusted himself off and was absolutely fine. 'He saved my life, and I always thought he was indestructible.'

Another *SNL* comedian who also owes a debt of gratitude to John Belushi is his brother, Jim. Following in his big bro's footsteps by becoming an actor himself, Jim said: 'There's an old saying: "When you drink the water, remember the men and women who dug the well". John dug the well for me.' He's also grateful to John's friends for taking care of him following the tragedy of losing his sibling: 'When my brother passed, Dan Aykroyd and John Candy just swooped in on me and they put their wings around me and healed me with love and attention.' In 2003, Jim and Aykroyd released their album *Have Love, Will Travel*, and still perform together at various venues across the US as The Blues Brothers.

Over the years, John has been remembered and revered. In 2004, he was posthumously honoured with a star on the Hollywood Walk of Fame. In 2015, *Rolling Stone* magazine ranked him as the greatest *SNL* cast member of all time, acknowledging that he was the 'live' in *Saturday Night Live*, the creative force who epitomized the ups and downs of the show.

Talking about Belushi's time on *SNL*, British comedian Nick Helm (who had a poster of the madcap star on the wall in his old flat) observed: 'You had this well-rounded cast and then you had this one guy who cut through everyone, and that was Belushi. Like Animal from The Muppets, he was everyone's favourite.' And in 2020, the documentary *Belushi* was released, with the tagline: 'Everyone loved him. Few knew him.' Directed by R. J. Cutler, it looks at his life as much as his death, and highlights not just the off-the-wall side of his character, but his gentler, sweeter side too. Love letters he'd written to his wife are included, and she seems happier that the world is now seeing her late husband in a different light. Now called Judy Belushi Pisano, she'd been disappointed with how Bob Woodward had outlined her husband's decline in his 1984 book *Wired: The Short Life and Fast Times of John Belushi*, and how this had come to define his memory. In an interview, she acknowledged that, although John wasn't perfect, he was loving, brave and kind-hearted. She loved that, as well as making people laugh, he also made them feel.

Chadwick Boseman

Age of death: 43

Date of death: 28 August 2020

Cause of death: Colon cancer

'You have to cherish things in a different way when you know the clock is ticking, you are under pressure.'

His Life

In an interview with *GQ* in 2015, Chadwick Boseman said ruefully: 'People don't make $140 million movies starring Black and brown people.' Fast-forward to 2018 and the man himself is starring in the $200 million *Black Panther*, which has a majority Black cast, Black writers, Black costume and production designers, and a Black director (Ryan Coogler). It was the first big-budget superhero film to be able to say this. Indeed, a lot can happen in three years. Between 2017 and 2020, Chadwick performed in seven films. During this time, while he was battling the American justice system (*Marshall*), Erik Killmonger (*Black Panther*), Thanos (*Avengers: Infinity War* and *Avengers: Endgame*), cop killers (*21 Bridges*), soldiers in the Vietnam War (*Da 5 Bloods*) and trailblazing blues singer Ma Rainey (*Ma Rainey's Black Bottom*), he – unbeknownst to his colleagues – was also battling cancer. Such was his work ethic and his desire for no fuss to be made, he showed up to film sets smiling, gave each character he played his all, and nailed every performance.

Prior to becoming a badass, box-office-smashing superhero, Boseman played real-life heroes in a selection of biopic flicks. He was National Football League (NFL) player Floyd Little in 2008's *The Express: The Ernie Davis Story*, before his breakthrough role in the 2013 film *42*, in which he played baseball legend Jackie Robinson. A year later, he was 'sex machine' James Brown in *Get On Up*, followed by civil rights lawyer Thurgood Marshall in the 2017 aforementioned *Marshall*. A running theme in these roles was people who had been the first African American to do something: Jackie Robinson was the first African American player in Major League Baseball, James Brown was the first Black American to own a private jet, and Thurgood Marshall was the first African American Supreme Court Justice. Boseman joined his comrades when he became the first Black actor to star in a Marvel superhero film. During his acceptance speech at the Screen Actors Guild Awards in 2019, surrounded by his castmates, he spoke of how being 'young, gifted and Black' meant they'd often been told there's no place for them, but that they knew they had 'something special to give the world'.

Chadwick's interest in the performing arts developed at high school. When a boy on his basketball team was shot and killed, Boseman wrote a play called *Crossroads* in response to the tragedy. It was performed at the school, and the 17-year-old realized that he liked telling stories. Throughout his career, he strived to work on projects that delivered the same emotional weight he felt when he lost his friend at such a young age. Boseman went on to attend Howard University in Washington DC, studying to become a director. Phylicia Rashad (most well-known as Clair Huxtable in *The Cosby Show*) saw something special in Boseman. 'What I saw in him was the sky was the limit,' she said. She became his mentor and, when the 'lanky young man with big eyes and an endearing smile' couldn't afford to attend the summer theatre programme he'd been accepted into at Oxford in England, she asked some of her friends, including Denzel Washington, to cover the cost. 'There is no Black Panther without Denzel Washington,' Boseman told the audience assembled to watch Denzel receive his AFI Life Achievement Award in 2019.

The BBC described Boseman as 'a film icon who changed Hollywood'. But even before he hit the big time, he was doing his darndest to change the perception of Black people on screen. At the age of 26, he was cast on soap opera *All My Children* as Reggie Montgomery, a teen thug with a drug-addict mother and absent father. When Boseman voiced his concerns to the show's writers about these racial stereotypes, he was fired just one week into the job being told he was 'too much trouble'. The role was recast with his future *Black Panther* co-star Michael B. Jordan.

Since then, 'trouble' hasn't been a recurring description of the star. Instead, he's been described as 'calm', 'a virtuoso', 'inspiring' and 'kind'. His kindness played out in his philanthropy, donating his time and money to causes such as the St. Jude Children's Research Hospital and the Jackie Robinson Foundation. He also donated $10,000 to the Boys and Girls Club of Harlem so that free tickets could be provided to children to watch *Black Panther*, and gave $4.2 million worth of personal protective equipment (PPE) to hospitals in Black communities during COVID. When discussing his career choices, Boseman once said, 'For me, doing this, it has to be meaningful.'

His Death

At the age of 43, on 28 August 2020, Chadwick Boseman died at his LA home with his wife and family with him. He had been diagnosed with stage III colon cancer in 2016, but it ultimately progressed to stage IV. Coincidentally, although Jackie Robinson Day is usually observed annually on 15 April, due to COVID it was marked on the same day Boseman passed away – seven years after he portrayed the baseball legend. The day after he died, Boseman's family announced his death on Twitter (now X), describing him as a 'true fighter'. The tweet became the most-liked tweet in history, with more than six million likes in less than twenty-four hours. By 31 August, it had over seven million. The third-most-liked tweet of all time is Barack Obama's 'No one is born hating another person because of the color of his skin or his background or his religion…', which he posted in 2017 and which received more than three million likes.

After Boseman's death, Obama paid tribute to the star, saying, 'Chadwick came to the White House to work with kids when he was playing Jackie Robinson. To be young, gifted, and Black; to use that power to give them heroes to look up to; to do it all while in pain – what a use of his years.' Many celebrities took to social media to express their devastation and pay their respects, including Oprah Winfrey, who said, 'What a gentle gifted SOUL. Showing us all that Greatness in between surgeries and chemo. The courage, the strength, the Power it takes to do that. This is what Dignity looks like'; and Jennifer Garner, who called him 'an artist, a scholar, a gentleman.' Denzel Washington released a statement, saying, 'He was a gentle soul and a brilliant artist, who will stay with us for eternity through his iconic performances over his short yet illustrious career.'

This illustrious career was celebrated even after his death. Boseman racked up masses of posthumous award wins and nominations for his roles as trumpet-playing Levee in *Ma Rainey's Black Bottom* and treasure-hunting Vietnam veteran in *Da 5 Bloods*. His Oscar nomination for *Ma Rainey's Black Bottom* made him the first ever Black performer to be nominated posthumously for an Oscar. Only seven actors have previously been nominated for the accolade after their death: Jeanne Eagels, James Dean, Spencer Tracy, Peter Finch, Ralph Richardson, Massimo Troisi and Heath Ledger. Chadwick's wife, Simone Ledward Boseman, accepted the Golden Globe he was awarded for his role in *Ma Rainey's Black Bottom*. In the acceptance speech, she tearfully declared, 'He would say something beautiful, something inspiring, something that would amplify that little voice inside of all of us that tells you you can, that tells you to keep going, that calls you back to what you are meant to be doing at this moment in history.' In 2022, Boseman also posthumously won the Primetime Emmy Award for Outstanding Character Voice-Over Performance for the *What If... T'Challa Became a Star-Lord?* television episode.

The day after Boseman died, Lewis Hamilton – the only Black driver in Formula 1 – won the Belgian Grand Prix. Standing on top of his race car, he performed the 'Wakanda salute', taken from the *Black Panther* films, which has become a symbol of Black strength and pride. In interviews after his win, Hamilton dedicated his triumph to Boseman, saying that he felt privileged to be able to 'shine some light onto an incredible legend and inspiring individual'. He expressed his extreme gratitude for what Boseman did for the Black community, and the wider world. 'As a young Black boy, I didn't have a superhero who I could look up to who was the same colour as me... This superhero shows all these young kids that it's possible... Wakanda Forever.'

A week after his death, on 4 September, a public memorial service was held in Boseman's hometown of Anderson, South Carolina. One of the speakers was James Brown's daughter, Deanna Brown-Thomas, who said, 'I looked at him as a younger brother, although he played my father... He is the epitome of Black excellence.' Several other people, organizations and ceremonies have honoured Boseman in their own way. Howard University's College of Fine Arts is now the Chadwick A. Boseman College of Fine Arts, in recognition of its former student. The 2020 MTV Video Music Awards was dedicated to Boseman. Various murals of – or inspired by – the star have popped up in a number of places, including New York, Dallas and Brixton, London. The 'King Chad' artwork was originally displayed in Downtown Disney in California but has since found its forever home at the Children's Hospital Los Angeles.

Simone continues to speak proudly about her husband. In an interview with Whoopi Goldberg for *Good Morning America* in November 2022, she talked about the scholarship that's been set up at Howard University in her late husband's honour. Sponsored by Netflix, the university offers the Chadwick A. Boseman Memorial Scholarship to students who, like Boseman, show exceptional skills in the arts. The first scholar to graduate, Shawn Smith, said, 'Chadwick Boseman's legacy has paved the way for me. He showed that you aren't just limited to these basic roles; you can do whatever you want.'

There's no denying that Boseman was a pioneer, a force for good, a game-changer. An article written about him in *The Guardian* said that 'he leaves the film-making landscape looking very different to how it was when he entered it.' And that 'Chadwick Boseman began his career playing African American icons and pioneers; he ends it as one himself.'

John Candy

Age of death: 43
Date of death: 4 March 1994
Cause of death: Heart attack

'I think I may have become an actor to hide from myself. You can escape into a character.'

His Life

It's hard to imagine anyone other than John Candy playing Uncle Buck. While Danny DeVito, Robin Williams, Jack Nicholson, Bill Murray, Jim Belushi, John Goodman and Tom Cruise (yes, really!) – who were all considered for the role – would have surely brought their own unique qualities to the part, it's doubtful they would have nailed it quite as perfectly as Candy, with his nutty humour, warm bonhomie and giant-pancake-flipping prowess. Minus the pancake flipping, the same could be said for his parts in *Planes, Trains and Automobiles*, *Cool Runnings, Who's Harry Crumb?* and *The Great Outdoors*. Even his supporting roles – like Tom Hanks' womanizing brother in *Splash*, an orange-whip-ordering parole officer in *The Blues Brothers,* and Gus the 'polka king of the Midwest' in *Home Alone* – saw the goofball comedian stealing the scene. Candy was only paid $414 for his memorable role in *Home Alone* (in contrast to his $350,000 salary for *Splash* and $800,000 for *Summer Rental*), turning down the offer of a slice of the film's profits from producer, screenwriter and friend John Hughes, saying instead that he would play the part as a favour. He was able to offer his services for one day of filming, which resulted in seventeen hours of hilarious improvising. 'The funeral-parlour story, that was all improvised at 4:30 in the morning,' recalled director Chris Columbus. 'We could barely keep a straight face on set just listening to John.' This favour cost the star millions, as the Christmas classic went on to make more than $476 million at the global box office. Candy appeared in eight films either written, directed or produced by John Hughes.

Whilst Candy was the perfect fit for all of these roles, there's one part that was originally written with him in mind that he didn't ultimately play… which was perhaps for the best. The part of Louis Tully in *Ghostbusters* – which ended up being played by Rick Moranis – was Candy's for the taking, but when he started offering suggestions that director Ivan Reitman wasn't keen on (like using a German accent and having a bunch of German Shepherd dogs), Candy turned the role down, realizing that their 'artistic differences' would be too great. Another of Moranis' characters – wacky Wayne Szalinski in *Honey, I Shrunk the Kids* – was also offered to Candy, but he declined it. Same story for Fred Flintstone in the 1994 *The Flintstones*, which ended up being played by John Goodman (alongside Rick Moranis playing Barney Rubble).

Candy's career began to take off in the mid-1970s when he was part of the comedy sketch show *Second City Television* (SCTV), along with the likes of other Canadian comedians Eugene Levy, Catherine O'Hara, Martin Short and the aforementioned Rick Moranis. Candy went on to win two Emmys for his writing on the show. After appearing in the 1981 *Stripes* with Bill Murray, the movie offers started rolling in. Candy quipped that instead of making do with macaroni and cheese, he could now afford to eat macaroni and lobster.

He performed in around forty-five movies, appearing in at least one a year between 1975 and 1994. On the whole, he played the funnyman – often a big-hearted loser or loudmouthed sidekick with a trademark chuckle – but in 1991, he stepped out of his comfort zone to play perjurious New Orleans attorney Dean Andrews in *JFK*. 'He worked so hard on that,' said Candy's daughter Jennifer. 'He had a dialect coach… He was so worried about it, getting that accent down.'

'Worry' isn't a word that immediately springs to mind when remembering John Candy. Instead, 'gregarious', 'lovable', 'generous' and 'hilarious' seem more accurate. However, he *did* worry. He worried about his health and his weight. Having lost his father to a heart attack when he was just 5 years old, Candy knew he was on borrowed time, saying as such on his fortieth birthday to *Only the Lonely* co-star Maureen O'Hara. It didn't help that he smoked a pack of cigarettes a day and enjoyed a drink or two. It was also reported that Candy used cocaine. He checked himself into the Pritikin Weight Loss Resort in Santa Monica, California for a month in 1984. He enlisted the help of personal trainers, began jogging, swimming and cycling, and went on diets – yet he struggled to balance his good intentions with his large appetite. He would eat well for a while, but the lure of buckets of shrimp and other unhealthy foods proved too much to resist. While his father's premature death encouraged him to strive for a healthy lifestyle, it also fuelled a sense of fatalism. If he was going to die anyway, what the hell, pass the perogies (which he developed a love for in 1991 when visiting Alycia's restaurant in Winnipeg in Canada, and would have shipped to the sets of his movies, plus to his home for Christmas, Thanksgiving and his birthdays). He felt that he had inherited a Damoclean sword, an impending doom, so whatever he did his fate was sealed. At the age of 40, Candy began having panic attacks, so sought help from a therapist. The actor grew tired of references to his size, with one critic referring to him as 'the elephant' in *Stripes*. In 1992, a hacked-off Candy backed out of hosting the Canadian Genie Awards after he watched the TV advert stating, 'We got the biggest star we could find'.

Candy was a generous soul, taking time to work with charities, including Make-A-Wish and the Elizabeth Glaser Pediatric AIDS Foundation. He always went out of his way to be kind – organizing surprise birthday cakes on set, learning every crew member's name and giving them a handshake and a 'thank you' at the end of the day, giving up his first-class seat on a flight to a weary camera assistant, arranging portable heaters and blankets at his own expense for those shivering during a long night shoot... *Planes, Trains and Automobiles* co-star Steve Martin said of Candy, 'He was a very sweet guy. Very sweet and complicated. He was always friendly, always outgoing and funny and nice and polite but I could tell he had kind of a little broken heart inside of him.' Despite his struggles, however, Candy had a happy family life. He married his wife Rosemary in 1979, after meeting on a blind date. They had two children, Jennifer and Christopher, who were 14 and 9 respectively when their dad died. The family lived on a twenty-acre farm in Queensville, Canada, with cats, dogs, cows and four Clydesdale horses: Peaches, Cream, Harry Crumb and Uncle Buck.

His Death

On 4 March 1994, while shooting what would be his final movie, *Wagons East*, in Mexico, John Candy, aged 43, suffered a fatal heart attack in his sleep. He'd had a great day on set and, after cooking a late-night pasta dinner for his assistants, had called his co-stars Richard Lewis and Robert Picardo to thank them. Picardo later said he was like a kid who'd had a fun day at camp.

The filming of *Wagons East* was completed using special effects and a stunt double, and was released five months after Candy died. It was dedicated to his memory, as was *Canadian Bacon*, his penultimate film, written and directed by Michael Moore. The 1998 *Blues Brothers 2000* was also dedicated to John Candy, as well as John Belushi and Cab Calloway, who all played significant roles in the original 1980 *Blues Brothers* movie.

Before his death, Candy had recorded a substantial amount of dialogue for the voice of a turkey named Redfeather for Disney's *Pocahontas*. Redfeather would have been Pocahontas' sidekick but, after Candy's death, the character was cut from the movie. Other roles that never came to pass for Candy were Ignatius J. Reilly in *A Confederacy of Dunces*, Atuk in *The Incomparable Atuk*, and Roscoe 'Fatty' Arbuckle in a biopic about the silent-film actor's life. All projects were ultimately shelved and labelled as 'cursed' because the actors who were in talks about playing these roles – John Belushi, Chris Farley, Sam Kinison and Candy – died before filming could take place.

Candy's funeral was held at St Martin of Tours Catholic Church on Sunset Boulevard in Los Angeles. Huge floral displays and banners reading 'Gentleman John', 'True Friend' and 'Uncle' surrounded the building. The funeral of Nicole Brown Simpson, OJ Simpson's ex-wife, was also held there a few months later. Some 200 mourners came to Candy's funeral, including Martin Short, Tom Hanks, Bill Murray, Chevy Chase, Rhea Perlman, Rick Moranis, Jim Belushi, Ed Harris and Eugene Levy. Levy likened his friend's absence to the air being sucked from the world. Sports executive Bruce McNall and ice hockey player Wayne Gretzky – who Candy co-owned the Toronto Argonauts football team with – also attended the service to pay their respects. (Candy was a huge sports fan, and his children recall their dad's three greatest passions in life being: his family, the Argonauts and his acting career – in that order.) Dan Aykroyd delivered the eulogy, during which he recited the lyrics of *O Canada*, the country's national anthem and 'John's favourite song'. Candy's funeral was deemed so important that the Los Angeles Police Department blocked off Interstate 405 – the busiest freeway in America – and escorted the procession. This had only ever previously happened for the funeral procession of President John F. Kennedy and when the Pope visited. 'Whenever I feel like I lose the importance of him to people, I just remember that happened,' said Candy's son. On 18 March, a memorial service for the star was held at St Basil's Church in Toronto, which was broadcast across Canada. *SCTV* and *Home Alone* co-star Catherine O'Hara delivered a moving tribute to her friend, sharing memories and anecdotes. Referring to Candy as the 'patron saint of laughter', she called him 'bright and quick and graceful and full of ideas', and said his movies were 'a safe haven for those of us who get overwhelmed by the sadness and troubles of this world.' She added, 'He left us a library of fun to remember him by.' Candy's final resting place is the mausoleum in Holy Cross Cemetery, his crypt lying above fellow actor Fred MacMurray's.

In 2006, Candy became one of the first entertainers honoured by Canada Post by being featured on a postage stamp, along with fellow Canadian actors Fay Wray, Lorne Greene and Mary Pickford. Toronto's mayor declared 31 October 2020 'John Candy Day', which would have been the actor's seventieth birthday. Rock band Ween dedicated their 1994 album *Chocolate and Cheese* to Candy. At the time, Gene Ween said, 'There was so much going on about Kurt Cobain [who died in the same year], and nobody mentioned John Candy at all. I have a special little spot in my heart for him.' Don't we all.

James Dean

Age of death: 24
Date of death: 30 September 1955
Cause of death: Car accident

'Live fast, die young, leave a good-looking corpse.'

His Life

Had it not been for James Dean, we may never have seen the likes of Robert De Niro, Johnny Depp, Leonardo DiCaprio or Nicolas Cage on the big screen. It was his handsome, brooding personification of teenage angst that inspired these now-accomplished actors, then-wide-eyed fans. Martin Sheen also credits Dean for his characterization of Kit in the 1973 *Badlands*. Elvis Presley may also never have swung his hips in such a provocative manner had it not been for the influence of Jimmy Dean. Comparing himself to the magnetic heart-throb, in a 1956 interview in *Parade* magazine, Presley said: 'We're sullen, we're broodin', we're something of a menace… That's what the girls like in men… I know you can't be sexy if you smile. You can't be a rebel if you grin.'

James Dean has become memorialized as the archetypal rebel, forever remembered for his portrayal of the moody, conflicted, passionate Jim Stark in the 1955 *Rebel Without a Cause*. It seems he enjoyed exuding a sense of daring, suggesting that trouble followed him around. Indeed, he embraced this image, even if it wasn't always true. His front two teeth were fake, as he had knocked them out as a child while swinging on a trapeze in his aunt and uncle's barn. He later said they'd been lost during a motorcycle accident. Fibber!

Far more films have been made about James Dean than he ever featured in himself. He only starred in three – *East of Eden, Rebel Without a Cause* and *Giant* – although he had walk-on parts in a handful of others, including *Has Anyone Seen My Gal?* and *Trouble Along the Way.* He also appeared in more than twenty television shows. *East of Eden* (for which he was cast as the lead over Paul Newman, who was deemed too old for the part) was the only film of his that he saw released in his lifetime; the other two were released posthumously. Dean became the first person to be officially nominated posthumously for an Oscar in the 1956 Academy Awards, for Best Actor in a Leading Role for *East of Eden*, then again for *Giant* a year later. He remains the only actor to have received two posthumous acting nominations. Not wanting to become typecast, his role in *Giant* (starring alongside Elizabeth Taylor and Rock Husdon) as a Texan ranch hand who strikes oil and becomes rich was a conscious career move to step away from the temperamental teen persona. His character, Jett Rink, was still pretty surly, though. For the later scenes of the film, Dean dyed his hair grey and shaved off some of it to give himself a receding hairline; sadly, the world never got to see how the actor would have aged for real.

Beginning his on-screen career at the age of 19, in a television advert for Pepsi-Cola in 1950 – for which he got paid $30 – it was clear that Dean had 'it': the X factor, star quality, charisma oozing from every pore. In *East of Eden*, much of his performance was unscripted, which resulted in some of the film's most moving scenes – like when Dean's character Cal hugs his father, crying, when the script had called for him to run away. He was also a talented theatre actor, starring in two Broadway plays, *See the Jaguar* and *The Immoralist*, in which he played a seductive, blackmailing, homosexual houseboy.

Dean was as enigmatic as his movie, TV and theatrical characters. His appeal knew no bounds and he is said to have had intimate relationships with women – such as Italian actress Pier Angeli, Swiss actress Ursula Andress and American actress Liz Sheridan – and men, like radio director Rogers Brackett, writer John Gilmore and screenwriter William Bast, who had been Dean's roommate at the University of California, Los Angeles (UCLA) and later in New York. Of his sexuality, Dean once said, 'No, I am not a homosexual. But I'm also not going to go through life with one hand tied behind my back.' Some believe his homosexual dalliances were a 'means to an end' to boost his career opportunities, while others think Dean was simply bisexual and having fun. Elizabeth Taylor concurred with the latter assumption: 'He hadn't made up his mind. He was only 24 when he died… He flirted around.'

Not only did Dean 'flirt around', he also raced around. Using his earnings to buy a silver Porsche (which he nicknamed 'Little Bastard'), he became an avid car racer, competing – and winning – in competitions such as the Palm Springs Road Races. So nervous were Warner Bros. studio of his need-for-speed hobby, it was written into his contract that he was banned from racing until he had finished shooting *Giant*. Turns out, their concern was warranted.

His Death

After Dean's death, Humphrey Bogart commented: 'Dean died at just the right time. He left behind a legend. If he had lived, he'd never have been able to live up to his publicity.' It's true that Dean left this Earth at the top of his game: young, attractive, successful… Had he not died, he may have gone on to star in B-movies and cringe-worthy sitcoms, he could have self-destructed down a drug-laden path, he could have given up the limelight to retire to Timbuktu… Or his star could have continued to rise and he could have been honoured with a lifetime achievement Oscar at the Academy Awards at the age of 98. We'll never know.

What we *do* know, however, is that on that fateful day, 30 September 1955 – a week after James Dean had finished shooting *Giant* – his Porsche Spyder was involved in an almost-head-on collision with a Ford Tudor just before sundown. His neck was broken, as were both his arms, his jaw was fractured and his foot crushed; he was pronounced dead on arrival at 6.20 pm at Paso Robles War Memorial Hospital. His passenger, Rolf Weütherich, a Porsche mechanic, was thrown from the vehicle and suffered head injuries and a broken leg, while the driver of the Ford walked away with only minor injuries. Apparently, Dean's last words to Rolf before the crash were: 'That guy's gotta stop… He'll see us.'

Ironically, Dean had filmed a public service announcement for the National Safety Council a few months before the accident, encouraging youths to slow down on the highway and be 'very cautious', just as he was. At the end of it, instead of saying the catchphrase 'The life you save may be your own', Dean had ad-libbed and said, 'The life you might save might be *mine.*' En route to a sports car rally in Salinas on 30 September, he had been pulled over by a police officer for speeding and cautioned to slow down. It was originally thought that he'd been travelling at 85 miles per hour at the time of the fatal collision but later reports, based on the wreckage and position of Dean's body, suggest it was more like 55 miles per hour.

Dean's funeral was held on 8 October 1955 at the Fairmount Friends Church in Fairmount, Indiana. Some 600 mourners attended, with around 2,400 fans gathered outside. The coffin remained closed due to the severity of the actor's injuries. He's buried at Park Cemetery just up the road, less than a mile from where he was raised on his aunt and uncle's farm, after his mother died when he was 9. The original tombstone and a bust of Dean were stolen – a rebellious act that perhaps had Dean smiling from his grave. A different bust of him now sits on the lawn of the Griffith Observatory in LA, which featured prominently in *Rebel Without a Cause*. The iconic 'HOLLYWOOD' sign can be seen in the background, causing much delight for camera-wielding tourists. The bust's artist Kenneth Kendall began working on the sculpture the night Dean was killed, and it was installed here in 1988. A replica of the bust can be seen at the James Dean Memorial Park in his hometown of Fairmount.

A junction near to the crash site has been named the James Dean Memorial Junction, and a makeshift memorial stands there, which includes a forever-changing array of items placed by fans – cigarettes, lighters, alcohol, pictures… About half a mile away, there's a permanent stainless steel monument wrapping around a tree, with James Dean's birth and death dates, an infinity symbol, and an inscription of a line from *The Little Prince* by Antoine de Saint-Exupéry: 'What is essential is invisible to the eye'. Underneath is a handwritten engraving from the aforementioned William Bast, who explains that this quotation was probably his friend's favourite, and that it seemed to 'hold a deep and private significance for him'.

Before Dean died, he had signed a six-year, nine-picture contract for $1 million with Warner Bros. He was set to have starred as Morgan Evans in a television dramatization of the play *The Corn is Green*, and boxer Rocky Graziano in the biopic film *Somebody Up There Likes Me*. As it turned out, Paul Newman (not deemed too old for *this* part) stepped into his boxing boots. According to *Forbes* magazine, James Dean's estate still earns around $5 million a year… and looks set to earn even more with upcoming projects. In 2019, it was announced that Dean would be 'brought back to life' with the use of computer-generated imagery (CGI) to star in his 'fourth film' *Finding Jack*, a Vietnam War movie. This bold move was met with controversy in the movie industry, with various actors tweeting their distaste. Chris Evans wrote: 'This is awful. Maybe we can get a computer to paint us a new Picasso. Or write a couple new John Lennon tunes…' But, according to director Anton Ernst, Dean's family was fully on board with the project and saw it as a movie he never got to make. Adding, 'We do not intend to let his fans down.' Despite being due for release on 11 November 2020 – Veteran's Day – the project was ultimately cancelled. A new film, *Back to Eden*, that uses AI to 'resurrect' James Dean is in production. When Dean was alive, he once said: 'If a man can bridge the gap between life and death, if he can live after he's died, then maybe he was a great man. To me, the only success, the only greatness, is immortality.'

Carrie Fisher

Age of death: 60
Date of death: 27 December 2016
Cause of death: Sleep apnoea and other undetermined factors

'No matter how I go, I want it reported that I drowned in moonlight, strangled by my own bra.'

Her Life

Sister Act. The Wedding Singer. Outbreak. Anastasia. Coyote Ugly. Mr. & Mrs. Smith. Made in America. My Girl 2. Lethal Weapon 3. All films that were made better by Carrie Fisher. Not because she acted in them, but because she tightened the scripts. As one of Hollywood's finest unsung 'script doctors' (working on more than twenty scripts throughout her career), the 1991 *Hook* can also be added to the list. Although, she did actually make a secret cameo in the film, alongside *Star Wars* creator George Lucas, where the pair are kissing on a bridge and float upwards when Tinkerbell sprinkles fairy dust on them. Lucas received an American Film Institute (AFI) Life Achievement Award in 2005, and Fisher concluded her hilarious speech at the ceremony with: 'I hope I slept with you to get the job, because if not, who the hell was that guy?' The 'job' she referred to was the role of Princess Leia. Signing up to play the sharp-tongued, 'cinnamon-bunned' character at the age of 19 in the 1977 *Star Wars*, the success of the movie meant that she went on to star in several subsequent films in the $70-billion franchise, the final one that she acted in being 2017's *Star Wars: Episode VIII – The Last Jedi*. In the same speech, Carrie made reference to her 'Leia-laden life' and admonished Lucas for not allowing her to wear a bra because 'there's no underwear in space'.

Fisher's sense of humour, candour and quick wit was a constant throughout her life and career – particularly in the books she wrote. Her last one – *The Princess Diarist* – is a memoir based on the diaries she kept around the time she starred in the first *Star Wars*. One of the revelations in the book is that she and co-star Harrison Ford had a three-month relationship. After this came to an end, she was briefly engaged to her *Blues Brother* co-star Dan Aykroyd (who proposed on the set of the film – and who also saved her life by performing the Heimlich manoeuvre as she choked on a Brussels sprout), but ultimately married singer-songwriter Paul Simon. His songs 'Hearts and Bones' and 'She Moves On' were inspired by their romance, and he wrote 'Graceland' after they divorced, which references their relationship. During the couple's marriage, Fisher appeared in her husband's music video for the ballad 'Rene and Georgette Magritte with Their Dog After the War'. Carrie went on to find a partner in talent agent Bryan Lourd, with whom she had a daughter, Billie.

Fisher wrote two other memoirs – one of which was *Wishful Drinking*, based on her one-woman theatre production of the same name, which she starred in. She also wrote four novels, which were semi-autobiographical, based around the struggles she'd had with addiction and her mental health. *Postcards from the Edge* was penned following an accidental overdose of prescription medication and sleeping pills, which saw her rushed to hospital. Fisher adapted the book into a screenplay (for which she was nominated for a BAFTA), and that became the 1990 movie starring Meryl Streep and Shirley MacLaine. When asked why she didn't play the part of the story's protagonist Suzanne (performed by Streep), Fisher replied that she'd already played Suzanne. As the two main characters were mother and daughter – both actresses – Fisher wasn't surprised when people asked her how closely the film paralleled the relationship of her and her famous mother, Debbie Reynolds.

The mother-daughter-best-friend duo – who lived next door to each other for fifteen years – starred in the 2016 documentary *Bright Lights: Starring Carrie Fisher and Debbie Reynolds*. But Fisher didn't just have a famous mother; she had a famous father too – singer and actor Eddie Fisher. (Carrie was 2 when her parents got divorced.) Her brother Todd acknowledged: 'My family, in particular, could overwhelm most people.' Carrie also had two half-sisters: actresses Joely Fisher, who played Paige in the 1990s sitcom *Ellen,* and Tricia Leigh Fisher, also an actress.

Whilst Carrie's most prolific role was Princess Leia, she also played many other characters throughout her almost-fifty-year career, acting in more than forty films, including: *When Harry Met Sally*, *The 'Burbs*, *Hannah and Her Sisters*, *Drop Dead Fred*, *Austin Powers: International Man of Mystery*, *Charlie's Angels: Full Throttle* and *The Women*. On the small screen, she was the voice of Angela in *Family Guy*, Rosemary Howards in *30 Rock* and Mia in the British comedy *Catastrophe*; the latter two roles saw her nominated for the Primetime Emmy Award for Outstanding Guest Actress in a Comedy Series. She made other guest appearances in *Sex and the City*, *Frasier*, *Entourage*,

Smallville, *Weeds* and *The Big Bang Theory*. Fisher wrote an episode for season nine of the sitcom *Roseanne*, titled 'Arsenic and Old Mom', which featured a guest appearance from Debbie Reynolds, who played Dan's (John Goodman's) mother, staying with the family after her release from a psychiatric hospital.

Fisher was very open about her own mental health and the fact that she had bipolar disorder. She gave nicknames to her bipolar mood swings: Roy, who was wild, and Pam, who sobbed a lot. Carrie/Roy/Pam featured in Stephen Fry's documentary, *The Secret Life of the Manic Depressive*, in which he described her as the 'poster child of manic depression', saying, 'She's on the edge of sanity… Not mad enough to be committed but not sane enough to lead much of a normal life.' In an interview with Oprah Winfrey, Fisher discussed her electroconvulsive therapy (ECT) treatments, which she would receive every six weeks to 'blow apart the cement' in her brain. She was also open about her alcoholism and addictions to cocaine and prescription medication. At her lowest point, she was taking thirty Percodan a day, using it to 'dial down' the manic element of her bipolar disorder. In a *Psychology Today* interview, Fisher explained that drugs made her feel more normal and 'contained' her. She was a supporter of several causes, including animal rights, women's advocacy and LGBTQ, and served as an honorary board member for the International Bipolar Foundation. Always aiming to destigmatize her condition with brutal honesty, she once said: 'I feel I'm very sane about how crazy I am.'

Fisher accomplished a great deal in her professional and personal life, but she always knew that, to most people, she was that gold-bikini-clad princess chained up by Jabba the Hutt. Said bikini sold for a whopping $96,000 (£63,000) at auction in 2015. She acknowledged that, come what may, she would always be seen as Princess Leia. 'Princess Leia will be on my tombstone.'

Her Death

Flying from London to Los Angeles on 23 December 2016, after finishing the European leg of her *The Princess Diarist* book tour, Fisher suffered a heart attack fifteen minutes before the aircraft landed. A passenger performed CPR on her and, upon landing, she was rushed to the Ronald Reagan UCLA Medical Center, where she was put on a ventilator in intensive care. Four days later, on the morning of 27 December, Carrie Fisher died, aged 60. The coroner ruled that the cause of death was sleep apnoea and 'other undetermined factors'. Traces of cocaine, heroin, morphine and MDMA were found in her system, but it's unknown as to whether these contributed to her passing.

The next day, Carrie's mother had a stroke and died. According to Todd, their mum's last words had been: 'I miss her so much. I want to be with Carrie.' A memorial service was held at the duo's property, with 125 guests in attendance, including Meg Ryan, Richard Dreyfuss, Gwyneth Paltrow, Stephen Fry, George Lucas and Meryl Streep. Streep led the mourners in a rendition of Fisher's favourite song, 'Happy Days are Here Again', which Carrie and her mother had performed together on *Oprah* in 2011. Both Fisher and Reynolds were laid to rest at the Forest Lawn Memorial Park in the Hollywood Hills. Fisher was cremated, while Reynolds was buried. Some of Carrie's ashes were placed inside her mother's coffin, and the remainder are held inside Carrie's favourite possession – a giant ornamental Prozac pill. 'She loved it,' explained her brother. '[Her daughter] Billie and I felt it was where she'd want to be.'

Fisher was nominated for and awarded many accolades posthumously, including a Grammy for the recording of her memoir audiobook *The Princess Diarist* in the Best Spoken Word Album category. In 2017, the release of *Star Wars: Episode VIII – The Last Jedi* was dedicated to Fisher, and she was made a Disney Legend in the same year. In 2019 – two years after her death – she appeared in *Star Wars: The Rise of Skywalker*, via the use of unreleased footage from *Star Wars: Episode VII – The Force Awakens*. Fisher's last acting role was as a witch, Hazel, in the coming-of-age fairytale *Wonderwell*.

In the days following Fisher's death, in the absence of a star on the Hollywood Walk of Fame, fans created their own memorial, adding the words: 'Carrie Fisher / May The Force Be With You Always / Hope' on a blank star. It was surrounded by candles, flowers, lightsabers, *Star Wars* figurines and cinnamon buns. Many mourners came to pay their respects dressed as their favourite *Star Wars* characters, including Chewbacca and Obi-Wan Kenobi. On May the Fourth – Star Wars Day – in 2023, Fisher was posthumously awarded an official star on the Hollywood Walk of Fame. When it was announced that a star would be bestowed on the actress, *Star Wars* co-star Mark Hamill took to Twitter (now X) to express his delight: 'Much love & a very special 1-finger salute to the incomparable, hilarious & irreverent force of nature that was my space sis Carrie Fisher. Her star will blaze from here to eternity.' Speaking at the ceremony, Billie – wearing a full-length dress with an image of Princess Leia on – said that her mother was 'glitter' and 'covered the world in it, both literally and metaphorically'. This referred to the fact that Carrie used glitter to bring both herself and others joy during dark times. Sprinkling some glitter on her much-missed mum's Hollywood star, Billie added, 'She left a mark of her sparkle on everyone she met.'

Clark Gable

Age of death: 59

Date of death: 16 November 1960

Cause of death: Heart attack

'On my tombstone they should write, "He was lucky and he knew it".'

His Life

'Go ahead, make my day'... 'Here's looking at you, kid'... 'I'll be back'... These are some of the most famous lines in movie history. Add to the list 'Frankly my dear, I don't give a damn', uttered by the devilishly suave Rhett Butler – played by Clark Gable – in the 1939 epic *Gone With the Wind*. Voted the number-one movie line of all time by the American Film Institute in 2005, it has been parodied in movies and TV shows galore – everywhere from Tim Burton's *Corpse Bride* to *The Toy* (starring Richard Pryor), *The Office* to *The Simpsons* to *Family Guy* to *American Dad*.

But it wasn't just this classic line that saw Gable leaving a lasting impression on the world of moving pictures. His name – along with actor Kent Taylor – was the inspiration for Superman's alter-ego Clark Kent. And Bugs Bunny owes his fast-talking, carrot-chewing traits in part to Gable's character in the 1934 *It Happened One Night*. In the romantic-comedy, Gable leans against a fence whilst chomping on carrots and talking with his mouth full. He also mentions a person named 'Bugs Dooley' and is referred to as 'Doc', suggesting inspiration for both Bugs' name and catchphrase 'What's up, Doc?' The beloved Bugs has appeared in more films than any other cartoon character, and even has his own star on the Hollywood Walk of Fame. As does Gable, who was awarded his on 8 February 1960, nine months before he died.

Hailed as 'The King of Hollywood', Gable appeared in more than eighty films throughout his almost-four-decade career and won an Oscar for his leading role in the aforementioned *It Happened One Night* (plus was nominated for his parts in *Mutiny on the Bounty* and *Gone With the Wind*). As well as a talented actor, he was also a decent human being. He almost walked off the set of *Gone With the Wind* when he saw that the facilities were segregated 'White' and 'Black'. He told the director that if the signs weren't removed, they wouldn't get their Rhett Butler. The signs were promptly taken down. Gable also planned to boycott the *Gone with the Wind* premiere in segregated Atlanta, as African American actors Hattie McDaniel and Butterfly McQueen were not allowed to attend. He only went after McDaniel pleaded with him to go. The pair also acted in *China Seas* and *Saratoga* together, and remained life-long friends. Hattie McDaniel was the first Black person to be nominated for and win an Oscar, as Best Actress in a Supporting Role for her character Mammy in *Gone With The Wind.*

With his trademark pencil-thin moustache, 6 ft frame and roguish smoulder, *Life* magazine described Gable as 'All man… and then some.' Not everyone agreed, however. Warner Bros. executive Darryl F. Zanuck said of the actor: 'His ears are too big and he looks like an ape.' Eccentric billionaire Howard Hughes famously quipped that Gable's ears made him look like 'a taxicab with both doors open.' But Gable's many leading ladies were only too happy to be cast multiple times alongside this 'big-eared ape/taxicab'. He made six films with Jean Harlow (including *Red Dust* and *Saratoga*, which she sadly died during the production of), seven films with Myrna Loy (including *Too Hot to Handle* and *Manhattan Melodrama*), four with Lana Turner (including *Homecoming* and *Betrayed*), eight with Joan Crawford (including *Possessed* and *Strange Cargo*), three with Norma Shearer (including *A Free Soul* and *Idiot's Delight*) and three with Ava Gardner (including *The Hucksters* and *Lone Star*). Another of Gable's leading ladies was Doris Day, who he starred with in the 1958 *Teacher's Pet*. Of her co-star, the actress said, 'He was as masculine as any man I've ever known, and as much a little boy as a grown man could be – it was this combination that had such a devastating effect on women.'

Indeed, Gable was married five times, and linked romantically to many other women, including Grace Kelly, Joan Crawford, Veronica Lake and Nancy Reagan (then Nancy Davis). Gable joked, though, 'Hell, if I'd jumped on all the dames I'm supposed to have jumped on, I'd have had no time to go fishing.' He did admit, however, that he had an eye for the ladies, but didn't necessarily prefer blondes, as he was accused of. He also found brunettes, redheads and even women with grey hair very attractive. For him, glamour had nothing to do with age, weight, height… or hair colour. He had a love child – daughter Judy Lewis – with actress Loretta Young, apparently conceived on an overnight train from a studio location in Seattle to Los Angeles, around the time they had been filming *Call of the Wild* together. Gable had been married to his second wife, Maria Langham, at the time. His third wife, actress Carole Lombard – who shared the screen with him in *No Man of Her Own* – was considered the love of Gable's life, and he never fully recovered after she tragically died in a plane crash after just three years of marriage. The pair affectionately referred to each other as 'Ma' and 'Pa', and lived on a ranch, dubbed 'The House of Two Gables' in Encino, Los Angeles. He described his marriage to the actress as 'a perfect thing', which he never expected to find again.

After Lombard's death, during World War II, Gable joined the US Army Air Force as an aerial gunner, flying various combat missions. During one, Gable's aircraft was damaged by flak, with some going through his boot and some narrowly missing his head. When word of this reached MGM, the studio asked the Army Air Force if their most valuable star could be reassigned to non-combat duty. For his bravery, Gable received many honours, including the Distinguished Flying Cross (DFC), the highest award for extraordinary aerial achievement. He also appeared in and narrated a propaganda film called *Combat America.* Hitler himself was so taken with the actor that he offered a hefty reward to anyone who could bring Gable to him unharmed.

Frankly my dears, this didn't happen. Thank goodness. Gable went on to make twenty-two more films after the war ended. His final being *The Misfits*, in which he played an ageing cowboy, and which was also Marilyn Monroe's last completed film before she died. The final scene sees the pair driving off together, with Monroe asking, 'How do you find your way back in the dark?' Gable replied, rather poignantly it turned out, 'Just head for that big star straight on. The highway's under it. It'll take us right home.'

His Death

The filming of *The Misfits* had been gruelling, with Gable insisting on doing many of his own stunts, one of which saw him dragged along the ground by a horse through the blistering Nevada desert. The other thing that left the actor the worse for wear was Marilyn Monroe, said to be exasperating on set. When filming finally wrapped, Gable expressed his relief that they were finished, declaring, 'She damn near gave me a heart attack!'

Two days later, while changing a tractor tyre, he suffered a coronary thrombosis and was taken to hospital by his pregnant wife, Kay. President Dwight D. Eisenhower sent Gable a telegram, instructing him, 'Be a good boy, Clark, and do as the doctors tell you to do.' Despite appearing to be improving, Gable died ten days after he had been admitted into hospital, on 16 November 1960, at the age of 59, after suffering another heart attack.

The Hollywood star was buried at Forest Lawn Memorial Park in Glendale, California, in a crypt next to Carole Lombard – his 'Ma' – in the Great Mausoleum. During their relationship, he had said, 'You can trust that little screwball with your life.' And there they lie together, in death. Kay had given her approval for her husband to be buried with Lombard and, five months later, gave birth to their son, John Clark Gable. He later followed in his father's footsteps to become an actor. Gable had previously said that if he ever had a child who went into acting, he'd turn in his grave. Oh dear. John's son – Clark James Gable, also known as Clark Gable III – was a host on the television show *Cheaters*, before he died from a drug overdose at the age of 30 in 2019.

John worked with the Clark Gable Foundation to help reconstruct the house in which his father was born in in Cadiz, Ohio, and convert it into a museum. Outside are handprints of *Gone With the Wind* cast members set into concrete. Inside is all manner of memorabilia, including photos, figurines, signed posters, crockery with Gable's face printed on and, of course, 'Frankly my dear, I don't give a damn' bumper stickers.

Gable has been portrayed in various films since his death. James Brolin played him in the 1976 *Gable and Lombard*, in which the trailer declares: 'His smile could break hearts, and box office records'. Larry Pennell played him in *Marilyn, The Untold Story*; Edward Winter in *The Scarlett O'Hara War*; Gene Daily in *The Rocketeer* and Charles Unwin in *Lucy*, to name a few. His name also cropped up in the 'Camelot Song' in *Monty Python and the Holy Grail*, and indie pop group The Postal Service produced a song named 'Clark Gable', released in 2003. In 1999, Gable was named the seventh greatest male movie star of classic Hollywood cinema by the American Film Institute, being pipped by Henry Fonda, Fred Astaire, Marlon Brando, James Stewart, Cary Grant and Humphrey Bogart.

'The King of Hollywood' never gave this title the time of day, describing the label as 'pure bullshit'. He didn't see that there was anything special about him that made him a star – 'I'm just a lucky slob from Ohio,' he said. Co-star, friend and on/off romance Joan Crawford disagreed. Ten years after he died, in an interview with David Frost, she said, 'He was a king wherever he went. He earned the title. He walked like one, he behaved like one, and he was the most masculine male that I have ever met in my life… Gable had balls.'

James Gandolfini

Age of death: 51
Date of death: 19 June 2013
Cause of death: Heart attack

'I like dark places.'

His Life

Hitman... Russian mobster... Stuntman... Navy lieutenant... Henchman... Mob enforcer... It's safe to say that, when it came to his roles, James Gandolfini had the tough-guy character nailed. He was best known for his performance as the ultimate tough guy, Italian-American mafia boss Tony Soprano in hit TV show *The Sopranos*. But, rather than just being a two-dimensional hard man, his characters had depth – they were complicated, flawed... human. One minute he'd leave viewers horrified at his criminal/adulterous/murderous behaviour, the next they'd be wanting to give him a hug. Tony Soprano paved the way for a new wave of antiheroes that allowed audiences to sympathize with protagonists who were corrupt, selfish, greedy, brutal, morally compromised, yet charismatic and relatable. Think Don Draper in *Mad Men*, Walter White in *Breaking Bad*, Dexter Morgan in *Dexter* and Jackie Peyton in *Nurse Jackie* (played by Edie Falco who, incidentally, played Tony Soprano's wife, Carmela).

The creator of *The Sopranos*, David Chase, described Gandolfini as 'almost a hippy', so it could be hard for the actor to go to the dark place Tony Soprano had to go to at times. To get into character, and channel Tony's rage, Gandolfini would use lack of sleep as a tool to make him angry. A few nights before a really violent scene, he'd make sure he'd only get two or three hours' sleep a night. He'd also put a pointy rock in his shoe and walk around on it all day, and bang his head on things – whatever it took to make him irate. It worked; *The Sopranos* became a cultural phenomenon, racking up (among other awards) twenty-one Emmys, five Golden Globes, two Peabodys and millions of viewers every week. During the show's final season, Gandolfini was being paid $1 million per episode, making him one of television's highest paid actors. In 2017, he was listed in *Entertainment Weekly* as the forty-second Greatest TV

Icon of All Time. *The Sopranos* ran for six seasons with eighty-six episodes, for eight years between 1999 and 2007. Before this huge success came many smaller roles, including that of Virgil, a philosophizing, woman-beating hitman in the 1993 *True Romance*. Now recognized as his breakthrough role, it was on the back of this that he was invited for an audition for the part of Tony Soprano, after casting director Susan Fitzgerald saw a clip. *True Romance* co-star Patricia Arquette said that he was very committed during shooting and, to stay in character, Gandolfini would sleep in his suit in his car.

But Gandolfini didn't just play the hard-ass; he was versatile. He did heartwarming (*Welcome to the Rileys*), he did comedy (*Surviving Christmas*), he did romance (*Enough Said*) and he did family adventure (*Where the Wild Things Are*). Heck, he even did an episode of *Sesame Street*, where he talked about being scared. He also did Broadway, starting his professional acting career in 1992 alongside Alec Baldwin and Jessica Lange in *A Streetcar Named Desire*; and earning himself a Tony nomination in 2009 for his performance in *God of Carnage*, in which he trod the boards alongside Jeff Daniels. Gandolfini took his talents behind the camera too, producing two emotive documentaries. Perhaps inspired by the fact that his father, James Senior, earned a Purple Heart in World War II, he wanted to help people understand the sacrifices that soldiers make. When the Iraq War was happening, he flew there with *Sopranos* co-star Tony Sirico (who played Paulie 'Walnuts' Gualtieri) to support the troops and let them know how much they loved and respected them for fighting. In *Alive Day Memories: Home from Iraq*, he interviewed injured Iraq War veterans, and in *Wartorn:1861-2010* – which had its premiere at The Pentagon – he explored the impact of post-traumatic stress disorder on soldiers and their families throughout various wars in US history. One of the soldiers talked afterwards about what a genuine guy he was, explaining that the interview had to be paused a couple of times because Gandolfini – or Jimmy, as everyone called him – started crying. After the interview, James asked the soldier, who had lost his legs, if there was anything he could do for him.

Other people who Gandolfini worked with talked of his big heart and generous spirit. When he got a raise during his time on *The Sopranos*, he shared the wealth by writing his co-stars cheques. Gandolfini wasn't always easy to work with, though. During the height of *The Sopranos*' success, sometimes he would simply not show up for work, causing much disturbance, worry and financial cost (closing down an airport for a shoot doesn't come cheap). He suffered from alcohol and cocaine abuse, meaning he could be temperamental, but those working with him decided this was a price worth paying in return for his phenomenal on-screen performance. Plus after some of his 'no-shows', he'd feel so guilty that he'd treat everyone on set to thoughtful gifts – once hiring a sushi chef for lunch or paying for everyone to get massages.

As well as being a kind colleague, he was a supportive friend. When John Travolta's 16-year-old son tragically died in 2009, Gandolfini flew to Florida to be with his good buddy, and wouldn't leave until he was sure Travolta would be OK (or as OK as one can be in such circumstances). When Gandolfini was a child in New Jersey, his father bought some tyres from John Travolta's father – little did they know, their kids' lives would become intertwined, going on to appear in six movies together, including *Get Shorty*, *Lonely Hearts* and *The Taking of Pelham 123*.

Former co-stars look back fondly on Gandolfini's mischievous sense of humour. Lorraine Bracco, who played Tony Soprano's therapist, once received a stuffed cockerel as a gift from him – or, as she recalls: 'He gave me this lovely *cock*.' Awarded the accolade of 'class flirt' in his senior high-school yearbook, Gandolfini liked to poke fun at himself and make people laugh. During the acceptance speech for his third Emmy as Lead Actor in a Drama in 2003, he said, 'To my son, Michael, I promised I would do this…' and then blew a raspberry into the microphone. When asked in an interview what he'd like God to say to him when he arrived at the pearly gates of heaven, the playful star joked, 'Take over for a while, I'll be right back.'

His Death

Gandolfini died of a heart attack on 19 June 2013, aged 51, whilst on holiday in Rome with his family – wife Deborah Lin, their 9-month-old daughter Liliana, and 13-year-old son Michael, from his first marriage. Michael found his dad in distress in the marble-covered bathroom of their suite (room 449) in Hotel Boscolo Exedra. Paramedics tried to resuscitate him, unsuccessfully, and then rushed him to Policlinico Umberto I Hospital, where doctors worked desperately to save his life. The actor was pronounced dead at 11 pm. At 6 ft 1 in and around 275 lb, Gandolfini was a big lad. He enjoyed his food, tucking into fried prawns and foie gras the night of his death. He had previously explained that his size helped him to play Tony Soprano to the best of his ability – '[Tony's weight] actually is important… When I do get thin… I don't feel the same, I don't walk the same… You know, with that lumber.'

Gandolfini had been in Italy to attend the Taormina Film Festival in Sicily, where he was set to receive an award and participate in a discussion about Italian-American views on cinema. Instead, a tribute was made to him, screening clips from his films and declaring that 'the secret of James Gandolfini and his appeal is that he had romance in his heart and in his eyes'. Three years earlier, in 2010, the Taormina Film Festival was connected to another sudden death caused by a heart attack: *Hollywood Reporter* film critic Peter Brunette died there whilst covering the festival.

The day after Gandolfini's death, Bruce Springsteen & the E Street Band, which has Steven Van Zandt (who played Silvio Dante in *The Sopranos*) as its guitar player, dedicated a performance of their album *Born to Run* to their friend Jimmy. His funeral was held on 27 June at the Cathedral of St John the Divine in Manhattan, which is also where Muppets creator Jim Henson's funeral was held in 1990, and where first lady and activist Eleanor Roosevelt's memorial was in 1962. David Chase gave a eulogy in the form of a letter to Gandolfini. He spoke about the fact that the star was so nice, patient and personal to strangers on the street, fans and photographers, adding: 'I also feel you're my brother because of the things we both loved. Family. Work. People in all their imperfection. Food. Alcohol. Talking. Rage... We amused each other.'

For his performance in the 2013 *Enough Said*, Gandolfini posthumously received much critical praise, several award nominations (including in the Screen Actors Guild Awards and the Critics Choice Awards) and won the Boston Society of Film Critics Award for Best Supporting Actor. His final role was in the crime drama *The Drop* (he died a month after shooting finished), for which he received positive reviews, with *Time* referring to him as 'Gandolfini the great'. Having worked on *Where The Wild Things Are* together, director Spike Jonze dedicated his Oscar-winning *Her* to Gandolfini after his death.

In 2014, James Gandolfini was inducted into the New Jersey Hall of Fame and, after a campaign by a high-school classmate, a section of Park Avenue in his hometown of Park Ridge was renamed James Gandolfini Way at a ceremony attended by crowds of his family, friends, co-stars and fans. In 2019, Gandolfini's son was cast as a young Tony Soprano in a prequel film to *The Sopranos* called *The Many Saints of Newark*. Set in 1967, the film follows the formative years of Tony and the other 'wise guys' of the show.

Following his death, tributes flowed from friends and co-stars, praising Gandolfini for his big heart, gentle soul and supreme talent. Dominic Chianese, who played Tony Soprano's Uncle Junior, likened the star to homemade wine. 'There are few like Jimmy – he was homemade wine: honest, good, pure, nothing added... Loyalty and truthfulness, that was him.'

Judy Garland

Age of death: 47
Date of death: 22 June 1969
Cause of death: Accidental drug overdose

'I believe in the idea of the rainbow. And I've spent my entire life trying to get over it.'

Her Life

At the age of 2-and-a-half, as she belted out 'When My Sugar Walks Down The Street' – then had to be physically removed by her father from the stage kicking and screaming, after three renditions – a star was born. That star – named Frances Ethel Gumm at birth, later to become Judy Garland in 1934 – was 'history's most poignant voice'. This voice has been described as effortless, brassy, velvety, powerful, resonant, vibrant, rich with emotion… It could pull you in, light you up, and break your heart. As demonstrated with what became Judy's signature song, 'Over the Rainbow' (which was almost cut from *The Wizard of Oz* as the sequence was initially thought too long).

But it wasn't just her voice that made Judy's star shine so bright – she was a 'triple threat', with a natural-born talent for singing, dancing and acting. She appeared in more than thirty-five films, with perhaps her most memorable role – Dorothy in *The Wizard of Oz* – featuring at the beginning of her career, at the age of 16. Her iconic blue and white gingham dress was selected for its blurring effect on her figure, somewhat disguising her teenage curves and making her appear younger.

Judy was never happy with her appearance, plagued by self-doubt and low self-esteem. The fact that she was dubbed an 'ugly duckling' by studio executives and 'my little hunchback' (she had a curvature of the spine) by MGM studio chief Louis B. Mayer didn't help – perhaps even caused the problem. Judy was constantly dieting, and was required to wear removable caps on her teeth and rubber discs to reshape her nose when posing for promotional photographs. Her insecurity followed her into adulthood and, despite a successful film and recording career, many awards (including the Academy

Juvenile Award in 1939; she remains one of only twelve people in history to have received the accolade), critical praise, her own Emmy-nominated TV series, and the ability to pack out Carnegie Hall with thousands of adoring fans, Judy always felt that she wasn't good enough. Audiences disagreed. They were awed by her charisma, magnetism and adaptability. They loved that she could belt out numbers in musicals such as *Meet Me in St. Louis, For Me and My Gal* and *Easter Parade* just as easily as she could make them laugh with her comedic roles in *Love Finds Andy Hardy* and *Andy Hardy Meets Debutante* (two of the ten films Judy starred in with Mickey Rooney), then turn on the drama in pictures like *The Clock* and *Judgment at Nuremberg*, for which she was nominated for an Academy Award for Best Actress in a Supporting Role. Another Oscar nomination was for the 1954 *A Star is Born* (remade in 1976 with Barbara Streisand and again in 2018 with Lady Gaga) for Best Actress in a Leading Role. So sure was the Academy that she'd win, they sent a camera crew to record her acceptance speech from the hospital where she had just given birth to her son. Alas, the award went to Grace Kelly for *The Country Girl*. Groucho Marx sent Judy a telegram stating that her loss was 'the biggest robbery since Brink's'. (The Great Brink's Robbery was an armed heist that took place in Boston in 1950, in which more than $2.7 million was stolen.)

Judy racked up five husbands, producing three children in the process – Joey Luft, Lorna Luft and Liza Minnelli. Lorna and Liza were chips off the old block, dancing, singing and acting like their mother (Lorna starred in *Grease 2* as the sexy Paulette; Liza became as legendary as her mum). Judy also racked up huge debts, owing the Inland Revenue Service (IRS) several hundred thousand dollars for not paying her taxes in 1951 and 1952. Liza was saddled with her mother's debts after her death.

At 4 ft 11½ in, Garland was a pocket rocket. She was headstrong, passionate, neurotic and volatile – traits not helped by her addiction to prescription drugs. Since her teens, she had become dependent on a cocktail of amphetamines and sleeping pills; alcohol was later added into the mix. She became unreliable, unstable… and unemployed. She was frequently late, increasingly erratic, repeatedly sued for backing out of performances and fired for not meeting contractual agreements. She was dismissed from the productions of *Annie Get Your Gun* and *The Barkleys of Broadway*. Audiences at her on-stage performances would boo and heckle her – sometimes even hurling bread rolls – when she forgot her lines after having kept them waiting for over an hour. Stevie Phillips, who had been Judy's agent for four years, described her as: 'A demented, demanding, supremely talented drug addict'. Countless suicide attempts (third husband Sid Luft said Judy had tried to take her own life twenty times in the thirteen years they were married) saw her in and out of psychiatric care. By the age of 23, Judy had had three nervous breakdowns.

But despite her troubles, Judy staged comeback after comeback. She would hit rock bottom, then dust herself off and hit the bigtime again after a spectacular recovery. This cycle was broken, however, when her body finally gave up. Her last film was the 1963 *I Could Go on Singing*. If only she had.

Her Death

'Judy... just plain wore out,' said Ray Bolger, who played the Scarecrow in *The Wizard of Oz*. On 22 June 1969, Judy was found dead in her rented house in London by her new husband Mickey Deans. She was 47. After climbing on the roof and smashing a window to gain access to the bathroom, Deans found Judy sitting on the toilet, with her head slumped forwards and her arms in her lap. Back in the US, in Kansas, a tornado struck the same day. The inquest found that she had died from an overdose of barbiturates (sleeping pills) but that it had not been intentional. The autopsy indicated that the drug had been taken over a long period of time, rather than in a single dose. It was believed that Judy also had an eating disorder, which contributed to her death.

Judy's body was transported to New York City where, a few days after her death, approximately 22,000 people paid their respects at the Frank E. Campbell Funeral Chapel in Manhattan, which was also the venue for the funerals of Heath Ledger, Joan Crawford, Joan Rivers and The Notorious B.I.G. The building stayed open all night to accommodate the vast crowd. The next day, on 27 June, the funeral took place, which was closed to the public and press. Stars attending included Katharine Hepburn, Sammy Davis Jr. and Lana Turner. Dressed in the gown she wore at her wedding just three months prior, Judy was then interred in a crypt at Ferncliff Cemetery in Hartsdale, New York. Nearly fifty years later, in 2017, at the request of her children, Judy's remains were reinterred at Hollywood Forever Cemetery in Los Angeles in a mausoleum named for her – the Judy Garland Pavilion. Another building named after her is the Judy Garland House in Hyannis Port, Massachusetts, where she would holiday with her friends President John F. Kennedy and his wife Jackie. Garland is said to have called the President every week, often concluding their phone calls by singing the first few bars of 'Over the Rainbow'.

The Hollywood icon also has a street on Studio Estates in Culver City, California named after her. Built on the former backlot of MGM Studios, this residential neighbourhood has a Garland Drive... as well as an Astaire Avenue and a Hepburn Circle. Another thing that bears the star's name is the Judy Garland floribunda rose. The yellow-petalled flower with orangey-red tips was bred in 1977 by Harkness Roses, after devoted fans searched for eight years to find a company willing to officially name a rose after their idol. It can be bought from various nurseries and is planted at the Judy Garland Museum in Grand Rapids, Minnesota. The museum includes her 1920s childhood home, restored and filled with memorabilia including the original carriage from *The Wizard of Oz*. One of the four surviving pairs of the famous ruby-red slippers worn by Garland in the film were stolen from the museum in 2005 but recovered via a sting operation by the FBI thirteen years later. In 2024, they went up for auction and sold for a staggering $28 million, making them the most valuable movie item ever sold at auction. The auctioneers described them as the 'Holy Grail of Hollywood memorabilia'.

Since her death, Judy has been depicted on screen many times. The 2019 biopic *Judy* saw Renée Zellweger scoop an Oscar, BAFTA, Screen Actors Guild Award – plus many other awards – for her portrayal of the star. In 1997, Judy herself was posthumously awarded the Grammy Lifetime Achievement Award. The Grammy Hall of Fame includes several of her songs, including 'Get Happy', 'The Trolley Song', 'Have Yourself a Merry Little Christmas' and 'Over the Rainbow', as well as her 1961 album *Judy at Carnegie Hall*. Garland was the first woman to win the Grammy Award for Album of the Year for this album, and the live concert recorded on it has been described as 'the greatest night in show business history'. Garland has also been depicted twice on US postage stamps: in 1989 as Dorothy from *The Wizard of Oz* and in 2006 as Vicki Lester from *A Star is Born*.

During her life, in the 1950s and 1960s, Judy became an icon in the gay community, always embracing such fans at a time when homosexuality was considered taboo (her father and two of her husbands – Vincente Minnelli and Mark Herron – were gay). The term 'friend of Dorothy' became slang for a gay man, used as a euphemism to discuss sexual orientation discreetly. The rainbow gay pride flag may have, in part, been inspired by Garland's most famous song. Her association with rainbows endures, and on 10 June 2022 – on what would have been Judy's one-hundredth birthday – the Empire State Building was lit up in rainbow colours to celebrate the star. Back in 1969, when Mickey Rooney learned of his co-star's death, he said: 'She was a great talent and a great human being. She… has found that rainbow. At least I hope she has.'

Corey Haim

Age of death: 38
Date of death: 10 March 2010
Cause of death: Pneumonia

'There's nothing I can say except a person's got to go through what they've got to go through.'

His Life

He was the 1980s heartthrob who, at the height of his fame, received 2,000 fan letters a week and spent his money on $300,000 cars. Having started acting at the age of 11, by the time he was 20, Corey Haim had a couple of TV series, two Young Artist Awards and more than ten films under his belt, including *Silver Bullet*, *The Lost Boys* and *License to Drive*. (In *License to Drive*, Haim was 16 and only had his learner's permit, so an adult had to hide on the backseat of the Cadillac when he drove it in the movie.) He was also offered the parts of Chris Chambers in *Stand By Me* and Charlie Fox in *The Mosquito Coast* (which both ultimately went to River Phoenix) but turned them down in favour of his starring role as the socially inept high-school student in the 1986 coming-of-age teen comedy/drama *Lucas*. For this performance, he received rave reviews, with esteemed film critic Roger Ebert writing: 'He creates one of the most three-dimensional, complicated, interesting characters of any age in any recent movie. If he can continue to act this well, he will never become a half-forgotten child star, but will continue to grow into an important actor. He is that good.' Sadly, though, like so many kids who grow up in the limelight, Corey Haim did become a half-forgotten child star, as well as a cautionary tale.

The Toronto-born actor admitted to drinking beer on the set of *Lucas* and trying marijuana at age 15 on the set of vampire romp *The Lost Boys*, which soon spiralled into a full-blown drug addiction to cocaine and crack, then later prescription drugs. His partner in crime – both on- and off-screen – was Corey Feldman, and 'The Coreys' became a commodity. The highest-paid teen stars in Hollywood, they enjoyed more fame, girls, money and good times than you could shake a string of garlic at. Throughout their careers, they starred in eight films together, including *The Lost Boys*, *Dream a Little Dream*, *National Lampoon's Last Resort* and *Busted*. In 2007, they also produced and starred in their own reality TV show, *The Two Coreys*. It was during this show that Haim confronted Feldman about the sexual abuse he endured at the hands of one of Feldman's acquaintances when he was 14 years old. He claimed Feldman had been aware of the abuse, which went on for two years. The pair had a public falling-out and *The Two Coreys* was cancelled halfway through the second season, with Feldman declaring, 'I am not going to watch him destroy himself', in reference to Haim's drug addiction.

But destroy himself he did. His attempts to get sober – with no less than fifteen stints in rehab – all ultimately failed and he branded himself a 'chronic relapser' with 'an addiction to pretty much everything'. He continued to work but, by the early 1990s, his drug addiction had taken its toll, and his performances and reliability were questionable. He was arrested in 1993 for wielding a replica handgun during a dispute with a business manager, and was sued for $375,000 in 1996 for pulling out of the movie *Paradise Bar*. Many of the roles he played were in direct-to-video films such as *Blown Away*, *The Double O Kid* and *Just One of the Girls*. Co-star in these movies and real-life fiancée Nicole Eggert said that on-set medics would be on hand to keep Haim from withdrawing. In the day, they would film together, then spend the nights at the hospital while Haim was hooked up to an IV, begging doctors for a different prescription, then they'd return to work the next day. Haim was also romantically involved with Victoria Beckham in 1995, before she rose to fame with the Spice Girls. Haim's drug use continued and, during the filming of *Busted*, which was Corey Feldman's directorial debut, he was fired by his best friend as he refused to try to get his addiction under control. Feldman later said this was one of the hardest and most painful things he had ever done.

Haim tried to regain his wholesome image by setting up a drug-advice hotline, but he later admitted that he was high while offering his 'don't-do-drugs' guidance. At the age of 26, after recovering from a drug-induced stroke, he filed for bankruptcy, having amassed huge debts and medical bills he was unable to pay. In 2001, Haim spent time in hospital as a result of his drug habit. In a bid to raise the funds to pay for his medical bills, he tried to sell clumps of his hair and an extracted molar on eBay. The tooth reached a price of $150 before it was removed by the company, so as not to breach eBay's rules about the sale of body parts. During another low point, a pawnbroker apparently witnessed Haim begging someone for $3 so he could buy a slice of pizza. Amidst all of this, Haim was still able to make fun of himself, popping up in a cameo performance in the 2003 *Dickie Roberts: Former Child Star*. During the end credits, Corey Feldman and Corey Haim look like they are having great fun as they sing: 'We don't know karate but we do know crazy; We'll beat you so bad your future will be hazy!' Other child stars who made an appearance in the film and have since also died too soon include: Dustin Diamond, Screech Powers from *Saved By the Bell*, who died aged 44 from lung cancer; Gary Coleman, Arnold Jackson from *Diff'rent Strokes*, who died aged 42 from a brain hemorrhage; and Jeff Conaway, Kenickie from *Grease*, who died aged 60 after an accidental drug overdose.

By July 2008, following *The Two Coreys* being cancelled, the once-fresh-faced teen idol was penniless and homeless in Los Angeles. Despite his trials and tribulations, however, Haim never stopped hoping to make the ultimate comeback. He continued acting in movies right up until his death, and had a number of projects in the pipeline that he never got to complete, such as the zombie flick *The Dead Sea*, on which he requested a 'clean set' to quell any drug temptation. 'I want to be the guy they talk about when they talk about comebacks,' he'd said. 'I want people to learn from me, see I'm human.'

In 2004, Haim was the subject of the song 'Whatever Happened to Corey Haim?' by Irish band The Thrills. The mellow tune, which became the year's most requested track on BBC Radio 1, highlights the fleeting nature of fame. At the time the question was posed, the answer could have been 'he got into drugs', 'he lost control' or 'he's planning a comeback'. Sadly, now, the answer is definitive and oh-so tragic.

His Death

Corey Haim died on 10 March 2010, aged 38, at Providence St Joseph's Medical Center in Burbank, California. Despite initial speculation that it was a drug overdose, he actually died from breathing complications related to pneumonia, and neither illegal nor prescription drugs were found to be a direct factor in his death. A small amount of eight drugs, however, were found in his system – some prescription, some over-the-counter and a tiny amount of marijuana. According to the autopsy report, Haim's heart was nearly twice the weight of a normal heart and some vessels were blocked as much as seventy-five per cent.

In the weeks prior to his death, an investigation found that Haim had been 'doctor shopping', using illegal aliases, to obtain at least 553 various prescription pills from different doctors, pharmacies, urgent-care facilities and emergency rooms. Reports concluded that he had procured thousands of pills during the last year of his life.

A private funeral was held on 16 March at Steeles Memorial Chapel in Thornhill, Ontario. A dozen fans waited outside, while 200 friends and family members attended the service. Corey Feldman did not attend but wrote an open letter to his friend, stating that his decision to stay away was to reduce the publicity for his family. He wrote, 'I always feared this day would come,' and reminisced, 'Nobody will ever understand the brotherhood we shared… Nobody will ever know how to do the secret Corey handshake… I pray that you are safe and warm and finally filled with peace. I love you.'

In March 2020, Feldman released his documentary *My Truth: The Rape of 2 Coreys*, in which he discusses the sexual abuse in Hollywood both he and Haim allegedly suffered in their teens. He had previously revealed that paedophiles in the movie industry were 'passing us back and forth to each other'. In the documentary, Feldman names one of the people who abused Haim as Charlie Sheen, alleging that a 19-year-old Sheen raped 13-year-old Haim while on the film set of *Lucas*. Sheen vehemently denies this, and Haim's mother does not believe it to be true. When Haim was still alive, he had suggested that he was scarred for life by things that had happened when he was a child.

Much upset was caused amongst Haim's family, friends and fans when he was omitted from the In Memoriam montage at both the Academy Awards and Screen Actors Guild (SAG) Awards in the year following his death. The media described it as a 'snub' and Haim's mother Judy said, 'The Academy Awards and [Screen Actors Guild] Awards totally forgot about my kid. It hurts me as a mother because they didn't give him the honour and recognition that he deserved.' Feldman was similarly disappointed: 'Corey dedicated his life to the film industry. The same industry that failed to dedicate even 30 seconds to his memory.' Although he may not have received a tribute at either of these high-profile events, Haim got one at the premiere of his final film, *Decisions*. Held at the Writers Guild Theater in Beverly Hills, amongst the famous faces were Alyssa Milano, who Haim dated in the late 1980s; his *The Lost Boys* co-star Jamison Newlander; and Sally Field, who starred with him in the 1985 comedy *Murphy's Romance*. Corey Feldman acted as master of ceremonies at the event, wearing a black jacket that Haim had given him, and describing the evening as a 'very bittersweet occasion'. In a previous tribute to his best friend, he had said, 'This is a tragic loss of a wonderful, beautiful, tormented soul.'

Anne Heche

Age of death: 53
Date of death: 11 August 2022
Cause of death: Car accident

'My life is a life movies are made of.'

Her Life

Anne Heche (pronounced 'Haysh') didn't like being pushed around. In 1997, she was told that if she took then-girlfriend Ellen DeGeneres to the premiere of her movie *Volcano*, she would lose her contract with film studio 20th Century Fox (now 20th Century Studios). Defiant, she took Ellen anyway… and was ushered out by security before the movie even ended, and told she couldn't go to the after-party for fear that photographs would be taken of the two women together. In a relationship for three years (from 1997 to 2000), Heche said that she and DeGeneres were 'part of a revolution' when it came to being loud and proud about who you could love. They were described as 'the first gay supercouple'. Ellen was the only woman Anne publicly had a relationship with, but she was also romantically involved with men, including Fleetwood Mac singer and guitarist Lindsey Buckingham (who wrote his solo song 'Down on Rodeo' about Heche), actor Steve Martin (who she met on the set of *A Simple Twist of Fate*), cameraman Coley Laffoon (who she married and had son Homer with) and actor James Tupper (who was her co-star in *Men in Trees*, and who she had son Atlas with). Some people thought that Anne dated Ellen for the fame/attention their relationship brought with it, with a *Saturday Night Live* skit portraying Anne as saying, 'I dated guys for years but no one even noticed'. It seems Anne didn't look back at her time with Ellen fondly and bad-mouthed her ex publicly some twenty years after their split. In her podcast *Better Together*, which she co-hosted with Heather Duffy and which ran from 2020 until her death, Anne said that Ellen was unkind and obsessed with money, emphatically calling her a 'bitch'.

A cute blonde, Heche's career could have gone the 'Meg Ryan' route. But romcoms weren't her thing; perhaps because she was openly dating a woman for a while, or perhaps because she had too much spunk to be typecast. Instead, the Ohio-born actress went for roles with more range. *The Guardian* film critic Peter Bradshaw said: 'The movies never really knew what to do with Anne Heche. Her gamine beauty and quizzically sharp intelligence were not easily absorbed into the Hollywood templates.' In the fifty-plus movies she acted in, Heche played everything from a presidential aide (the part was originally written for a man) in *Wag the Dog*, to a New York magazine editor lost in the jungle with Harrison Ford in *Six Days, Seven Nights*, to a seismologist in *Volcano*, to a loner living in the woods in *I Know What You Did Last Summer*, to a distressed wife of an undercover FBI agent (played by Johnny Depp) infiltrating the mafia in *Donnie Brasco*. The latter was considered her breakthrough role, with *The New York Times* writing that 'Heche does well with what could have been [a] thankless role'.

Heche also dabbled with directing, working on projects like *If These Walls Could Talk 2, Ellen DeGeneres: American Summer Documentary* and *Reaching Normal* (all of which starred DeGeneres). She wrote and directed *Stripping for Jesus*, a dark comedy in which a stripper writes Bible verses on her body before she goes on stage. Heche commanded the Broadway stage, acting in productions such as *Proof* and *Twentieth Century*, for which she was nominated for a Tony Award. She won over the small screen, too; in fact, it's where her career began. In 1987, she played 'evil twins' Vicky Hudson and Marley Love in *Another World*, which saw her winning a Daytime Emmy Award. After that, she appeared in many other television series, including *Ally McBeal*, *Nip/Tuck*, *Everwood*, *Men in Trees*, *Hung*, *The Brave*, *Dig*, *Chicago P.D.* and – perhaps unsurprisingly – *Ellen* (although here she's only credited as 'Woman at Next Table'). To add to her eclectic characters, Heche also played Marion Crane in the 1998 remake of *Psycho*, recreating the iconic shower scene. And the mentally ill mother of infamous serial killer Jeff Dahmer in *My Friend Dahmer*. The positive reviews she received for this role included the words 'brilliant', 'unforgettable', 'quirky' and 'oddly fun'. When talking about this film on the *Megyn Kelly TODAY* show, Heche said that she herself 'was raised in a very difficult family and that's part of why [she] needed to play Joyce Dahmer'.

Difficult was right. Anne's parents were fundamentalist Christians (which she subsequently likened to being 'raised in a cult') and moved the family eleven times during her childhood. In her memoir *Call Me Crazy*, Heche wrote about the extensive sexual abuse she suffered at the hands of her father. He was a closeted homosexual and ultimately died from AIDS-related complications when Anne was 13 years old, despite telling his family that he had cancer.

When Anne began dating Ellen, Anne's deeply religious mother was not happy, saying, 'I am dumbfounded, in a state of shock. Doesn't Anne know what homosexuality has done to our family?' Tragedy struck Anne's siblings, with three of them dying before she did: sister Cynthia at 2 months old from a heart defect, brother Nathan at 18 from a car crash three months after their father died (Anne believed the accident to be suicide), and sister Susan at age 48 from a brain tumour. Heche was estranged from her remaining sibling, Abigail, for many years but eventually reconciled. Anne never did reconcile with her mother, however. After claiming in her memoir that her mother was aware of the abuse she endured as a child, Nancy Heche responded by saying she found 'no place among the lies and blasphemies in the pages of this book'.

Anne talked openly about her struggles with mental health, explaining that she went through a period when she heard God speaking directly to her, who told her that she had an inner being named 'Celestia'. During this time, she claimed to have had experiences with clairvoyance, automatic writing, speaking in tongues, having stigmata appear on her feet, and faith healing. In 2000, Heche, wearing a bra and shorts, abandoned her car and walked to a rural home in Fresno, California. Here, she tried to persuade the residents to board a spaceship destined for heaven with her. Police picked her up and she was taken to a psychiatric hospital. Heche said that she was 'insane' for the first thirty-one years of her life as a result of the childhood abuse she suffered. But she said that she wrote *Call Me Crazy* 'to say goodbye, once and for all to [her] story of shame and embrace [her] life choice of love… Happy freedom Anne. You have made it to the other side'.

Her Death

On 5 August 2022, Heche drove her car – which was travelling at around ninety miles per hour – into a house, sparking a fire, which blazed for over an hour and took fifty-nine firefighters to extinguish. She was trapped inside her Mini Clubman for forty-five minutes, suffering smoke inhalation and severe burns in the process. The actress was taken to the Ronald Reagan UCLA Medical Center for emergency care, and then to Grossman Burn Center at West Hills Hospital, where she remained in a coma for several days. On 11 August, she was declared brain dead, which, in Californian law, means a person has officially died. Heche, aged 53, was kept on life support for three days as it was her wish to be an organ donor and recipients had to be located. Hospital staff lined the corridors to hold an 'honour walk' in recognition of the fact that Anne was donating her organs and saving lives in the process. Her family said in a statement: 'Today we lost a bright light, a kind and most joyful soul.'

Prior to Heche's fatal crash, she'd had two other motoring scrapes in the Mar Vista neighbourhood in LA on the same day – one striking an apartment garage and one hitting a Jaguar and failing to stop. Video footage shows her to be driving at great speed, at one point nearly hitting a pedestrian. This sequence of events led officials to initially believe that she had been under the influence of alcohol or drugs. But the results of her autopsy revealed that she was not impaired by any substances when the accidents took place, and that no active drugs were found in her system.

Heche had completed shooting a number of films that were yet to be released when she died. One of which was *Girl in Room 13*, which is dedicated to Anne's memory (co-star Larissa Dias described her as 'a firecracker'). Heche had four movies come out in 2023, including horror flick *You're Killing Me* – in which she played a fiercely protective mother – and the family feel-good *Wildfire,* where she was a rodeo trainer, and in which she performed her own stunts. She had also written a follow-up memoir to *Call Me Crazy*, titled *Call Me Anne*, which was released posthumously.

Many of Anne's co-stars offered their condolences on social media, with Robert DeNiro saying: 'I'm very sad to hear of the tragic passing of Anne Heche. She was a wonderful actress and I enjoyed working with her tremendously in *Wag the Dog*. Sad! Sad! Sad!' Alec Baldwin – who Anne trod the boards with on Broadway and starred with in the 2023 *Supercell* – posted a video on Instagram, calling her 'a pal' and 'a very special comet shooting across the sky.' Ellen tweeted: 'This is a sad day. I'm sending Anne's children, family and friends all of my love.'

Anne Heche's funeral was held nine months after her death, on 14 May: Mother's Day. Stars such as Rosanna Arquette, Heather Graham and Eva La Rue attended. Heche's son Homer said, 'We are convinced our mom would love the site we have chosen for her. It's beautiful, serene and she will be among her Hollywood peers.' Said site is the Hollywood Forever Cemetery's Cathedral Mausoleum, and the Hollywood peers her cremated remains were laid to rest amongst include Mickey Rooney, Barbara La Marr, Peter Lorre, Rudolph Valentino and Burt Reynolds. Anne's memorial plaque reads: 'Mother, actress, writer, director, creator, believer. Live in love.'

Philip Seymour Hoffman

Age of death: 46

Date of death: 2 February 2014

Cause of death: Drug overdose

'I think you should be serious about what you do because this is it. This is the only life you've got.'

His Life

Pudgy. Weak-jawed. Dishevelled. Philip Seymour Hoffman certainly didn't cut a figure of your typical leading man. But, my goodness, could he command a screen. His career spanned around twenty-five years – one of his first acting gigs being on an episode of *Law & Order* in 1991, playing a man accused of rape – and in that time, he appeared in more than fifty films. Whether he was playing a spoiled student (*Scent of a Woman*), a wacky storm chaser (*Twister*), a worried nurse caring for a dying man (*Magnolia*), a priest accused of paedophilia (*Doubt*), a charismatic cult leader (*The Master*), a rogue disc jockey (*The Boat That Rocked*), a villainous arms dealer (*Mission Impossible III*), a talented violinist (*A Late Quartet*), an ailing theatre director with an ambitious vision (*Synecdoche, New York*), a flamboyant drag queen (*Flawless*), or one of his other many varied characters, he certainly made an impression with each and every performance. Typecast he was not! He brought a convincing depth to every portrayal, sprinkling his characters with as much pathos, gravitas or humour as required, whether he was in a supporting role or the protagonist, in an independent film, a Hollywood blockbuster or a cult classic (such as *The Big Lebowski* or *Boogie Nights*). Although most of his characters were far from endearing – a collection of weirdos, misfits, creeps, bullies, pedants, degenerates, sad sacks, losers, idiots and, in the case of Allen in *Happiness*, a persistent masturbator ('I didn't go out looking for negative characters; I went out looking for people who have a struggle and a fight to tackle') – you can't help but feel sympathy for them because Hoffman somehow makes them real, complex and vulnerable.

As it was, Hoffman himself was real, complex and vulnerable, too. In his early twenties, he drank heavily and used heroin. At 22, he checked himself into rehab. He got clean and remained sober for twenty-three years but, sadly, slid back into his addiction in 2013. It seems the rush he got from acting (in a 2006 interview on *60 Minutes*, he'd likened performing live on stage to a drug that becomes addictive) was no longer enough and he sought another 'fix'. Mimi O'Donnell – his partner and mother of their three children (Cooper, Tallulah and Willa) – attributes his relapse partly to the death of his longtime therapist and also a falling out he had with some of his Alcoholics Anonymous (AA) friends. She thinks that his love-hate relationship with acting could also have contributed to his downfall – he deeply loved acting but hated the lack of anonymity it brought. He described acting as 'torturous' and trying to be great as 'absolutely torturous'.

But great he was. Lauded as one of the most admired and ambitious actors of his generation, Hoffman was adept at playing people with addictions – perhaps drawing on his own experiences to get inside each character's head. In *Before the Devil Knows You're Dead*, he played a devious realtor desperate to support his drug habit; in *Owning Mahowny* he was an embezzling bank employee with a gambling addiction; on stage, he played an alcoholic in *Long Day's Journey into Night*, and an ex-heroin addict in *Shopping and Fucking* in 1998. Anthony Minghella, who directed Hoffman in *The Talented Mr Ripley* and *Cold Mountain*, recognized the actor's creative battles: 'Philip is an extraordinary actor, cursed, sometimes, by his own gnawing intelligence... He struggles for every moment in a film, overthinks, overanalyzes, wrestles with the scene.'

This overthinking, overanalyzing and wrestling always seemed to pay off. As well as commanding the silver screen, Hoffman also commanded the stage, both on and off-Broadway. He joined the LAByrinth Theater Company in 1995, where he directed, produced and acted in many stage productions until his death. He also served as an artistic director there for some time. He was nominated for a Tony Award for his performances in three Broadway plays: *True West* in 2000, *Long Day's Journey into Night* in 2003, and *Death of a Salesman* in 2012. He played the same lead, Willy Loman, in his high-school production of *Death of a Salesman* in 1984.

Hoffman became well-versed at taking to the stage to deliver an acceptance speech, racking up a plethora of awards for his work, both in theatre and on the big screen. Most notably, he took home a Best Actor Golden Globe, BAFTA, Oscar and many other film-industry awards for the biographical movie *Capote* in 2006. Audiences and critics alike were bowled over by his performance, not least because he altered his voice and appearance dramatically (losing a lot of weight to shrink into Capote's delicate frame and mimicking his soft drawl) to convey the famously effeminate writer Truman Capote. Capote wasn't the only real-life character that Hoffman played, though. He also depicted music journalist Lester Bangs in *Almost Famous*, baseball team manager Art Howe in *Moneyball*, and CIA operative Gust Avrakotos in *Charlie Wilson's War*. For the latter, he was nominated for an Academy Award for Best Supporting Actor (he was also nominated in the same category for his performances in *Doubt* and *The Master*). When Hoffman collected his Academy Award for *Capote*, he thanked his mother for raising him and his three siblings on her own, and for taking him to see his first play. Said play was Arthur Miller's *All My Sons*, which Hoffman watched when he was 12 years old. He was transfixed and later said, 'I was changed – permanently changed – by that experience. It was like a miracle to me.'

His Death

Hoffman died of a drug overdose on 2 February 2014, when he was 46 years old. The New York medical examiner's office stated that his death had been caused by acute mixed drug intoxication, including heroin, cocaine, benzodiazepines and amphetamines, and that it had been accidental. Hoffman's friend, David Bar Katz, found him with a syringe in his arm in his apartment in Greenwich Village. Police later found around seventy bags of heroin in the same apartment. After his critically acclaimed play *Death of a Salesman* finished its run, Hoffman had started to use the drug again. He apparently injected twice as much heroin daily as a typical addict. On the afternoon of Hoffman's death, more than 100 people gathered outside the building to pay their respects to the actor.

The funeral was held five days later at the Roman Catholic Church of St Ignatius Loyola, which is where the funerals of first lady Jacqueline Kennedy Onassis, and singers Lena Horne and Aaliyah were also held. Among the 400 mourners at Hoffman's funeral were many of the Hollywood elite, including Meryl Streep, Cate Blanchett, Ethan Hawke, Spike Lee, Michelle Williams, Laura Linney, Julianne Moore, Joaquin Phoenix, John Slattery, Jerry Stiller, Marisa Tomei, Amy Adams and John C. Reilly.

The LAByrinth Theater Company honoured their longtime friend and collaborator with a candlelit vigil outside the theatre, and Broadway dimmed its lights for one minute. Three weeks after Hoffman died, Katz set up the American Playwriting Foundation in his friend's memory. Using the money awarded from a libel lawsuit against the *National Enquirer,* which had wrongly said that Hoffman and Katz were lovers, the foundation established the Relentless Award. It awards an annual sum ($45,000 initially, increased to $65,000) to the writer of an unproduced 'challenging, fearless, passionate, relentlessly truthful, not mainstream' play. All characteristics that can be attributed to the late, great Hoffman himself.

Another tribute for the star was from fellow actor and friend Sam Rockwell, who dedicated his Oscar for *Three Billboards Outside Ebbing, Missouri* to him. 'For my old buddy, Phil Hoffman,' he said, raising his golden trophy in the air. And Cate Blanchett, who starred with Hoffman in *The Talented Mr Ripley*, dedicated her BAFTA for *Blue Jasmine* to her much-missed friend. During her acceptance speech, she said that Hoffman had been 'a continual, profound touchstone' for her and 'a monumental presence who is now so sadly in absence'. She spoke of his talent, generosity and 'unflinching quest for truth', concluding with: 'Phil, buddy, this is for you, you bastard, I hope you're proud.' During the 2014 Academy Awards ceremony, the In Memoriam segment included images of Hoffman, along with Paul Walker and James Gandolfini. Gandolfini and Hoffman had appeared together at the second Annual LAByrinth Theater Company Celebrity Charades: The Rematch at The Roxy in New York in 2004. A photo of them at this event can be found on Instagram, with fans of the two actors expressing their heartache with comments like: 'They're doing exactly this in heaven right now' and 'Too much talent in one picture'.

Shortly before his fatal overdose, Hoffman had filmed the pilot episode of TV show *Happyish*, a dark comedy that saw him playing a discontented advertising executive. Those working on the show recall how the star's assistant would supply him with a constant stream of sugar-based foods, a common craving for users of heroin. Following his death, the role went to Steve Coogan. Hoffman was also gearing up to start work on his second directorial movie project (his first being the 2010 *Jack Goes Boating*, which he also starred in), a Prohibition-era drama called *Ezekiel Moss*, which was to star Jake Gyllenhaal and Amy Adams. Hoffman died during the filming of *The Hunger Games: Mockingjay – Part 2*, playing Plutarch Heavensbee, a game maker turned revolutionary. He had completed most of his scenes but some digital trickery and script tweaking was needed to complete the film, so the audience didn't notice his absence. It may have worked, but moviegoers have certainly noticed his absence since, yearning for the devastating performances he never got to play in the acclaimed movies he never got to be in.

Whitney Houston

Age of death: 48

Date of death: 11 February 2012

Cause of death: Accidental drowning, caused by heart disease and cocaine use

'I'm looking forward to the years to come. Good years.'

Her Life

To say that Whitney 'The Voice' Houston was 'kind of a big deal' in the entertainment industry would be like saying that Mother Teresa was 'quite a nice lady'. The New Jersey-born singer, songwriter, actress, film producer, philanthropist and all-round legend is recognized by the Guinness World Records as the most-awarded female artist of all time, winning a whopping 400-plus awards throughout her triumphant career. Having a plethora of genres in her repertoire – including pop, R&B, soul, rock, rock and roll, gospel, dance, funk, disco, hip-hop, Latin pop, house, opera and new jack swing – means she has been inducted into numerous halls of fame, including the Grammy Hall of Fame, Rock & Roll Hall of Fame, New Jersey Hall of Fame, Georgia Music Hall of Fame, Songwriters Hall of Fame and National Rhythm & Blues Hall of Fame. She released seven studio albums and two soundtrack albums, all but one of which have been certified diamond, multi-platinum or platinum. *The Bodyguard* soundtrack, released in 1992, became the first album in history to sell more than a million copies in one week when it first came out, and remains the highest-selling soundtrack of all time, shifting 45 million copies worldwide. Houston's signature song, 'I Will Always Love You', sat comfortably at number one on the Billboard Hot 100 chart for fourteen consecutive weeks, and remains the best-selling single by a female artist.

But it wasn't just her voice that could bring you to tears with a single syllable that earned the superstar her success. Houston could also command a screen – as proved by her roles in *The Bodyguard*, *Waiting to Exhale*, *The Preacher's Wife*, *Cinderella* and *Sparkle*. For her role in *The Preacher's Wife*, Houston earned

$10 million, meaning she was the highest-paid African American actress in Hollywood at the time. Her soundtrack for this film sold more than six-million copies worldwide, making it the best-selling gospel album ever. The *Waiting to Exhale* soundtrack was nominated for eleven Grammys, with Houston's 'Exhale (Shoop Shoop)' scooping the Grammy for Best R&B song. Wanting to also be involved behind the scenes in the movie business, Houston set up the film-production company BrownHouse Productions, and produced a handful of films, including *The Princess Diaries*, *The Princess Diaries 2*, *The Cheetah Girls*, *The Cheetah Girls 2*, and the aforementioned *Cinderella* and *Sparkle*. *The Princess Diaries* made more than $165 million, which meant that Houston and her business partner Deborah Martin Chase became the first Black people in history to produce a film that surpassed $100 million at the box office. Houston's career could have taken a different route, however. In the early 1980s, she was offered the role of Sondra or Denise Huxtable in *The Cosby Show*, but turned it down to focus on her music career.

The 1995 *Waiting to Exhale* (directed by Forest Whitaker) reached number one at the US box office, grossing $81.5 million worldwide. Houston said that the movie was 'a breakthrough for the image of Black women because it presents them both as professionals and as caring mothers'. The unlikely hit broke down stereotypes, portraying its lead cast of four African American female friends as strong middle-class citizens. Although the cast was all-Black, the audience transcended ethnic boundaries, appealing to all races. The same can be said for Houston's music. When she first hit the mainstream, she was slated by some Black disc jockeys for being 'too white' and 'not having soul', but she responded by saying that she doesn't know how to 'sing Black' or 'sing white', she just knows how to sing. 'Music is not a colour to me. It's an art.' She also declared that she knows what colour she is, having been raised in a Black community.

She was also raised surrounded by music. Her mother was Cissy Houston, the Grammy-winning soul and gospel singer; her cousins were successful singers Dionne and Dee Dee Warwick; another cousin was opera singer Leontyne Price; her godmother was singer Darlene Love; and 'Queen of Soul' Aretha Franklin was her 'honorary aunt'. Whitney began her career at the age of 14, when she would perform as a backing singer for her mother's band in Manhattan cabaret clubs. She gave her first solo performance during Cissy's set at Manhattan's Town Hall in February 1978, singing 'Tomorrow' from the musical *Annie*, for which she received her first standing ovation. Family was extremely important to Whitney, who once said that if everything wasn't right with her family then nothing would be right. The shocking revelation in the

2018 documentary *Whitney* that her cousin Dee Dee Warwick molested her as a child horrified Cissy, with her and Dionne Warwick releasing a joint statement calling the claim 'unfathomable' and 'rumour, innuendo and hearsay'.

Houston's mother instilled a strong faith in her daughter and brought her up to be a proud, generous Christian. Not only did Whitney Houston have the voice of an angel, when it came to charity and helping others, she behaved like one, too. In 1989, she established the Whitney Houston Foundation for Children, which fought to prevent child abuse, taught children how to read, granted college scholarships, built inner-city parks and playgrounds, and offered medical assistance to sick and homeless children. She donated money to various charities, including the United Negro College Fund (UNCF), St. Jude Children's Research Hospital, and Harlem's Hale House Center, which cared for babies who were born addicted to drugs. After performing 'The Star-Spangled Banner' at the 1991 Super Bowl, she donated all of her earnings for the sale of the single to Gulf War servicemen and their families through the American Red Cross Gulf Crisis Fund. Likewise, when she re-released the anthem after the September 11 terrorist attacks, she waived her royalty rights, and the money raised – which amounted to more than $1 million – went to the New York Firefighters 9/11 Disaster Relief Fund and the New York Fraternal Order of Police organization.

When Whitney married singer Bobby Brown on 18 July 1992, she thought she'd found her happily ever after, but their fourteen-year marriage, before they divorced in 2007, was highly publicized as being tumultuous, abusive and awash with drugs. Scenes of the pair arguing aired on the reality television show *Being Bobby Brown.* Comedian Eddie Murphy, who Whitney dated in the mid-1980s, is said to have called his ex on the morning of the wedding to try to convince her she was making a mistake. Brown recalls seeing his bride-to-be before the ceremony hunched over a bureau, snorting a line of cocaine. Although he declined to partake on that occasion, the couple took drugs together countless subsequent times.

They had a daughter, Bobbi Kristina, who would be looked after by nannies in one wing of their house while her mum and dad got high in another. Despite this, she was her parents' pride and joy, with Whitney embracing motherhood, saying, 'My daughter is my greatest inspiration.' In a 2009 interview with Oprah Winfrey, Houston spoke candidly about the couple's drug use, saying that their 'drug of choice' was weed laced with rock cocaine. She said that by the time she made *The Preacher's Wife*, she was using drugs everyday 'trying to hide pain'. She acknowledged that she was so in love with Bobby that 'he was [her] drug'. During this time, her professional life suffered. She'd show up hours late for interviews, rehearsals and photo shoots, would cancel concerts, and was even fired from singing at the 2000 Academy Awards due to her failure to perform well or take direction during rehearsals. She tried multiple stints in rehab in an attempt to get clean, to no avail.

In a similarly heartfelt and honest interview in 2002, with Diane Sawyer, Houston was asked what she would like her ideal life to look like in ten years' time. She said she'd like to be retired, watching her daughter grow up as a faithful follower of God, one day having children of her own. Whitney definitely saw grandchildren in her future. She declared: 'I am not a person who wants to die. I am a person who has life and wants to live.'

Her Death

On 11 February 2012, Whitney Houston, at age 48, was found face-down and unconscious in the bathtub in her suite at The Beverly Hilton hotel by her assistant. Paramedics were called and performed CPR but were unable to revive her. Houston's cause of death was stated as accidental drowning caused by the 'effects of atherosclerotic heart disease and cocaine use'. The drug was found in her system, along with marijuana, anti-anxiety drug Xanax, muscle-relaxant Flexeril and allergy-medication Benadryl. She also had a build-up of plaque in her arteries, a condition common in drug users. Houston's death coincided with the 54th Annual Grammy Awards ceremony, which was held the next day, and which included a tear-jerking tribute to the star, with Jennifer Hudson singing 'I Will Always Love You'.

Houston's funeral was held on 18 February at the New Hope Baptist Church in New Jersey, where she sang as a child. It was an invitation-only service, with around 1,500 family and friends in attendance, including Mariah Carey, Oprah Winfrey, Chaka Khan, R. Kelly, Brandy, Forest Whitaker and Jennifer Hudson. Whitney's family allowed the service to be recorded and streamed online for her many fans to watch. Musical tributes from Stevie Wonder, who admitted to the congregation that he'd had a 'little crush' on Whitney, and Alicia Keys, who sang 'Send Me an Angel', punctuated the eulogies given – notably by record producer Clive Davis, actor and filmmaker Tyler Perry, Dionne Warwick, and Whitney's co-star in *The Bodyguard,* Kevin Costner. Costner referred to her as 'the sweet miracle of Whitney' and talked about the fact that when he worked with her on the movie, she suffered from self-doubt and worried that she wasn't good enough. He said, 'If you could hear me now, I would tell you you weren't just good enough, you were great... You weren't just pretty, you were as beautiful as a woman could be. And people didn't just like you, Whitney.

They loved you.' He spoke directly to Whitney's daughter Bobbi Kristina twice throughout his speech, and encouraged her to 'sing [her] heart out'.

Tragically, three years later, Bobbi Kristina was found in eerily similar circumstances to her mother: immersed and unresponsive in a bathtub with drugs in her system. In a coma for six months, she succumbed to the lobar pneumonia she had developed from the incident and died on 26 July 2015, at the age of 22. Both Whitney and Bobbi Kristina are buried at Fairview Cemetery in Westfield, New Jersey, next to Whitney's father.

Whitney may no longer be with us, but her memory and her music live on. And then some. In October 2020, her 'I Will Always Love You' music video surpassed one billion views on YouTube, making her the first solo artist of the twentieth century to reach this milestone. Her 1987 hit 'I Wanna Dance With Somebody (Who Loves Me)' had been streamed on Spotify a billion times as of 2023, and her single 'Higher Love', which was released posthumously, reached this feat in 2024. In October 2023, Houston was named by Guinness World Records as the highest-earning dead female celebrity. But her estate doesn't just *make* money, it also *raises* money for good causes. As a continuation of the Whitney Houston Foundation for Children, the Whitney E. Houston Legacy Foundation was formed in 2020, and helps young people to rebuild their lives and restore their self-esteem.

Houston's final film, *Sparkle*, was also released posthumously, six months after she passed away. Inspired by the true story of 1960s girl group The Supremes, she played the mother of three sisters who struggle with fame and drug addiction. Given how everything turned out for Whitney, the poignancy of the film's subject matter becomes ever more highlighted when her character asks her daughters: 'Was my life not enough of a cautionary tale for you?'

Rock Hudson

Age of death: 59

Date of death: 2 October 1985

Cause of death: AIDS-related complications

'Someone asked me once what my philosophy of life was, and I said some crazy thing. I should have said, "How the hell do I know?"'

His Life

Tall, dark and ridiculously handsome, Rock Hudson was the all-American dreamboat. Except… he wasn't. Although men wanted to be him and women wanted to marry him, the star's public, clean-cut image was a far cry from who he actually was in 'real life'. Born Roy Harold Scherer Jr., he changed his name to Rock Hudson (after the Rock of Gibraltar and the Hudson River) at the insistence of his agent, Henry Willson. Willson was key in developing the 'beefcake' craze of the 1950s and shaped Hudson into the charismatic hunk who lit up the screen and set women's hearts aflutter. The fact that he was gay was an open secret in the movie industry. In some of his films, double entendres – such as Leslie Caron's character telling him, 'Hiding in closets isn't going to cure you' in *A Very Special Favor* – suggested that he was happy to be in on the nudge-nudge-wink-wink jokes. But to those outside this inner circle, Hudson remained firmly in the closet for most of his life. Had he not, it would have been career suicide.

And what a career it was! One of the most popular film stars of his time, Hudson was a big hitter during the Golden Age of Hollywood and beyond. Despite the fact that he struggled to remember his lines (it famously took him thirty-eight takes to successfully deliver his one line in his first movie *Fighter Squadron*), between 1948 and 1984, he was in nearly seventy movies, including the 1956 *Giant*. He was nominated for an Oscar for his role in this movie, as was his co-star James Dean. Alas, they both lost out to Yul Brynner for *The King and I*. Hudson didn't stick to one movie genre. He did romantic comedies (*Come September*), action flicks (*Ice Station Zebra*), musicals (*Darling Lili*), dramas (*Magnificent Obsession*), war films (*A Farewell to Arms*), westerns (*The Undefeated*), science-fiction pictures (*Seconds*) and disaster movies (*Avalanche*). He even tried his hand at horror films (*Embryo*). Hudson also shone on the small screen, in shows such as crime drama *McMillan & Wife* (during which time he was the highest paid star on television) and soap opera *Dynasty*, which was his final role. Not bad considering his shaky start into the world of acting. His screen test for 20th Century Fox (now 20th Century Studios) was so terrible that the studio showed it to young actors for decades as an example of how they too could become a star if they worked hard enough, no matter how bad their performances were to start with.

Among his leading ladies were Elizabeth Taylor, Mia Farrow, Julie Andrews and Doris Day (who he starred in three films with: *Pillow Talk*, *Lover Come Back* and *Send Me No Flowers* – 'I just loved working with him. We laughed and laughed,' she said). Whilst many actors would be thrilled to be paid to lock lips with such beauties, women simply didn't float his boat. He liked men… but homosexuality was taboo in the 1950s, and it certainly wouldn't have landed him any film roles. To keep up the pretence of being the quintessential straight moviestar and quash any rumours about his sexual orientation, Hudson married Willson's secretary, Phyllis Gates, on 9 November 1955. Although, for him, the union was purely transactional, she married for love and filed for divorce after three years, citing mental cruelty.

Between 1962 and 1965, Hudson had a secret relationship with then-film extra Lee Garlington, who Hudson referred to as his true love. Garlington described Rock as a kind, respectful gentle giant (at 6 ft 4 in), loved by everyone who worked with him. Hudson was also romantically linked to many other guys, including actors Anthony Perkins, Errol Flynn and Marlon Brando, musician Liberace, comedian Jim Nabors, novelist Armistead Maupin (who outed Hudson as gay during the last few weeks of the actor's life) and Tom Clark (who published the memoir *Rock Hudson: Friend of Mine*).

Following years of heavy drinking and smoking, Hudson had a heart attack in November 1981. Needing emergency quintuple heart bypass surgery, he recovered. But his health took a turn for the worse when he was diagnosed with AIDS in June 1984. The following year, he let the world know what he was battling and was bombarded with love and support, receiving 28,000 letters from fans, telegrams from dozens of celebrities – including Frank Sinatra, Richard Dreyfuss and Madonna – and a phone call from President Reagan. Hudson was one of the first celebrities to disclose his AIDS diagnosis and the unexpected response was incredible. People's attitudes shifted: AIDS was no longer seen as a 'filthy' disease but as one that could be contracted by one of the world's most-loved film stars. Actress Morgan Fairchild said that Rock Hudson 'gave AIDS a face'. Joan Rivers also applauded Rock's courage, saying that when she'd previously hosted a benefit for AIDS, she couldn't get any major stars to turn up. Rock's admission brought AIDS to the public's attention and helped millions of people in the process.

The shock revelation that he had the illness sparked widespread public discussion and an increase in the funding of medical research. Hudson himself donated $250,000 to amfAR (American Foundation for AIDS Research), helping to launch the non-profit organization, which his friend and co-star Elizabeth Taylor became Founding National Chairperson for. In September 1985, the Hollywood AIDS benefit Commitment to Life was held, and Hudson – too ill to attend – sent a telegram, saying: 'I am not happy that I am sick. I am not happy that I have AIDS. But if that is helping others, I can at least know that my own misfortune has had some positive worth.'

His Death

On 2 October 1985, at the age of 59, Rock Hudson died at his home in Beverly Hills from an AIDS-related illness. He was the first major celebrity to die from the disease, and the news made international headlines. It was his wish that there was no funeral, but he was cremated and a cenotaph later constructed at Forest Lawn Cemetery in Cathedral City, California. His ashes were scattered at sea, from a yacht, twenty-five miles from the Los Angeles mainland, where he loved to sail. Hudson wanted fifty people to be present, including Elizabeth Taylor, actor Roddy McDowell and film producer Stockton Briggle. According to Yanou Collart, a publicist and friend of Hudson's, he then wanted 'a big party with mariachis and champagne'. After Hudson's ashes were scattered, a rainbow appeared. 'We all just stood there and tried to comprehend that such a thing could have happened,' said Briggle. 'So, Rock's ashes went out to sea, surrounded by a huge rainbow. That was finally how he was put at peace.'

Contributions for AIDS research and the care of AIDS sufferers continued to flood in. Congress set aside $221 million to develop a cure for the illness, and over $1.8 million in private contributions (more than double what was raised in 1984) was collected since Hudson had made his announcement. Hudson's proceeds from his memoir *His Story* – co-written by Sara Davidson and drawing on interviews from close friends and colleagues, family scrapbooks and letters – went to the Rock Hudson AIDS Foundation, a fund within the aforementioned amfAR. Indeed, Hudson changed the course of history surrounding AIDS.

But not everyone gave money in Rock's honour; some took it. Hudson's former boyfriend, Marc Christian, sued his estate on the grounds of 'intentional infliction of emotional distress' as Hudson had failed to disclose that he had AIDS, despite the fact that the couple were still having sex. Christian discovered the truth from a news report. He also sued Hudson's personal secretary, Mark Miller, for $10 million because he claimed that Miller had lied to him about Hudson's illness. A jury awarded Christian $21.75 million in damages, which was subsequently reduced to $5.5 million. Later, it appears Christian forgave his former lover by defending Hudson, saying that how he'd behaved was out of character. Robert Park Mills, the lawyer who represented Hudson's estate against Christian, wrote a book called *Between Rock and a Hard Place: In Defense of Rock Hudson, From the Ashes of Trial to the Light of Truth*, in which he questions Christian's allegations.

This lawsuit inspired the theatre production *Playing Rock Hudson*, with other plays – such as *Rock* and *Hollywood Valhalla* – also being made about the star. Hudson's memory also lived on in the 1990 film *Rock Hudson*, the 2020 Emmy Award-winning TV show *Hollywood* (Hudson is played by Jake Picking), Kelly Clarkson's song 'Rock Hudson', and the 2023 documentary *Rock Hudson: All That Heaven Allowed* (the title a take on his 1955 romantic drama *All That Heaven Allows*). In this revealing biography, various people who Hudson had worked with were interviewed, including *Dynasty* co-star Linda Evans. She reflected on the on-screen kiss that Rock had given her after he'd been diagnosed with AIDS, before going public with the news. It was supposed to be a passionate embrace but he had delivered a prim, closed-mouth smooch, much to the show's producers' chagrin. They decided to reshoot the scene a week later, hoping for a steamier outcome, to no avail. Nobody, least of all Linda, could understand why Hudson was holding back… but when he revealed that he had AIDS a few months later, it all made sense. At the time, in the mid-1980s, much fear surrounded the disease and people believed it could be transmitted via saliva. In *All That Heaven Allowed*, Linda talks of her anger towards the people who accused Hudson of being cavalier with her health: 'I saw how hard he tried to protect me.' Some of these cast and crew members refused to be on set with her, for fear that she had contracted the disease. She was never worried that she had AIDS and described Hudson as a 'delightful human being', who was 'funny and deep and kind and charming'. At the end of the documentary, Hudson himself quotes the novelist and poet George Eliot: 'Nobody really dies until they're forgotten.'

Heath Ledger

Age of death: 28

Date of death: 22 January 2008

Cause of death: Accidental overdose

'Life is so short. It's like we're already gone, really, in retrospect.'

His Life

The glitz, the glamour, the fame, the money: none of it appealed to Australian actor Heath Ledger, named after Heathcliff in Emily Brontë's *Wuthering Heights*. A self-confessed introvert, the limelight wasn't a place he enjoyed. But, ever since catching the acting bug at age 10 when he starred as Peter Pan in his school play, he loved to perform, and being a celebrity was the price he had to pay to do it. In a career cut short, this self-taught actor was in twenty films, each carefully selected by him. It would have been all too easy for the tall, attractive star to have gone down the 'dreamboat' route after his first big movie role in *10 Things I Hate About You* (in which he was selected over Josh Hartnett and Ashton Kutcher) in 1999. Indeed, blockbuster offers came his way – including the role of Spider-Man – but Ledger refused to become a film studio's commodity. After a meeting that discussed billboards, tours, paydays and campaigns, he recalled feeling like a bottle of Coke and excused himself from the group of executives to have an anxiety attack in the bathroom. Being a movie star didn't sit comfortably with Ledger and he wasn't motivated by the pursuit of stardom – he was driven by the desire to disappear into a character. In a 2006 interview with *Rolling Stone* he stated that he deliberately '[took] the blond out of [his] career', choosing anything-but-squeaky-clean roles, such as a volatile skateboarding mentor in *Lords of Dogtown*, a suicidal prison officer in *Monster's Ball* and an artistic heroin addict in *Candy*.

He made gutsy choices, purposely pushing the envelope to test himself – and his audience. This was never more evident than with his role as Ennis Del Mar in *Brokeback Mountain*, in which he played a gay cowboy. '[Cowboys] are the very symbol of American masculinity,' said friend and fellow Australian actor Ben Mendelsohn in the documentary *I Am Heath Ledger*. 'This is one of the biggest heartthrobs on Earth taking on that character. That's balls. And that's an artist.' Despite shying away from the spotlight, the success of this romantic tragedy thrust Ledger slap-bang into the centre of it, where he scooped an armful of awards, including the MTV Movie Award for Best Kiss, with co-star Jake Gyllenhaal. Ledger was also nominated for an Academy Award, a BAFTA and a Golden Globe, being pipped for all three by Philip Seymour Hoffman for his performance in *Capote*. Ennis wasn't the first gay character Ledger had portrayed, however. In 1996, he played Snowy Bowles, a gay cyclist in the TV series *Sweat*. A year later, he was (straight) local bad boy Scott Irwin in *Home and Away*, one of Australia's most successful television shows.

It was on the set of *Brokeback Mountain* that Ledger met and fell in love with Michelle Williams, who played his long-suffering on-screen wife. Prior to this, he'd had relationships with actresses Naomi Watts (his co-star in *Ned Kelly*) and Heather Graham. Williams and Ledger had a daughter, Matilda Rose, in 2005 but split up – reportedly because of Ledger's heroin and cocaine abuse – when she was 2 years old. Ledger was allegedly no stranger to drug use, apparently stating in a video that he used to smoke five joints of cannabis a day for twenty years. He suffered from bouts of chronic insomnia, so turned to prescription drugs to help him sleep. Some suggested that playing the Joker in *The Dark Knight* took its toll on the actor's mental health but Ledger was quoted as saying, 'It's the most fun I've had playing a role'. After he and Williams split up, Ledger was romantically linked to supermodels Helena Christensen and Gemma Ward, and actresses Kate Hudson, Lindsay Lohan and Mary-Kate Olsen.

Ledger also produced and directed music videos, including Ben Harper's 'Morning Yearning' and Grace Woodroofe's cover of David Bowie's 'Quicksand'. Ledger and Harper started the record label Masses Music together and signed Woodroofe, mentoring her through the start of her career. Ledger had aspirations of being a film director and, before he died, had been preparing for the shoot of *The Queen's Gambit*, the story of a drug-addicted chess prodigy, set to star himself and Ellen Page (now Elliot Page). The film adaptation of *The Queen's Gambit* never came to fruition but it went on to be made into a television series, released in 2020, that won multiple awards, including eleven Primetime Emmys and two Golden Globes. There's no way to know how Ledger would have fared as a movie director but we do know that as an actor, he was insanely gifted, fearless and utterly mesmerizing.

His Death

Heath Ledger was found dead in his New York apartment by both his masseuse and housekeeper on 22 January 2008, at the age of 28. On finding the body, his masseuse called Mary-Kate Olsen, before dialling 911. Olsen's bodyguards arrived on the scene around the same time as the paramedics. The autopsy found various different prescription drugs in Ledger's system, including Valium, Xanax, oxycodone, hydrocodone, temazepam, doxylamine – a lethal combination of painkillers, sleeping pills and anti-anxiety medication. A DEA investigation took place to ascertain where Ledger had obtained all of the drugs – with Olsen being subpoenaed as she initially refused to cooperate with police – but no charges were filed and the case was closed, despite the origin of two of the drugs remaining unknown. It was declared that Ledger had died from an accidental overdose.

His funeral was a private affair held in his hometown of Perth, Australia, attended by family and close friends, including ex-fiancée Michelle Williams, who read out Shakespeare's 'Shall I Compare Thee to a Summer's Day?' A memorial service was also held, with around 500 mourners in attendance, including Ledger's ex-girlfriend Gemma Ward, and fellow Australian actors Bryan Brown and Cate Blanchett. Blanchett, who co-starred with Ledger in *I'm Not There*, gave an emotional eulogy, remembering the times the pair had spent together in New York and Los Angeles. Later in the year, at the Independent Spirit Awards, the star dedicated her award for Best Supporting Actress for *I'm Not There* to Ledger, describing him in her acceptance speech as 'probably one of the most beautiful independent spirits of all'. The week after Ledger died, Daniel Day-Lewis dedicated his Screen Actors Guild Award to the actor, calling the portrayal of his troubled character in *Monster's Ball* 'unique' and his performance in *Brokeback Mountain* 'perfect'.

At the time of Ledger's death, he had been part way through filming fantasy film *The Imaginarium of Doctor Parnassus*. Initially, writer and director Terry Gilliam thought that production would halt and that Ledger's performance as Tony would never be seen… but then, amidst the grief of losing a friend, he had a brainwave. He adapted the script and cast Ledger's friends Johnny Depp, Jude Law and Colin Farrell in the movie, each playing 'fantasy transformations' of Tony. Of being part of the film, Farrell said, '[It] was never about filling Heath's shoes as much as seeing them across the finish line.' The three actors gave their wages from the film to Ledger's daughter, Matilda. On completion of the movie, Gilliam changed part of the credits from 'a Terry Gilliam film' to 'a film from Heath Ledger and friends'. Other cast and crew members created their own tribute to Ledger, in the form of a heart-shaped tattoo. The star had written a note with his email address on and scrawled a heart on it. This heart was replicated and became a permanent feature on Verne Troyer's hand, Lily Cole's wrist and Holly Gilliam's (Terry's daughter's) arm. Lily Cole, who played Ledger's love interest in the film, said on Instagram: 'A heart drawn by someone who reminds me daily to wear my heart on my sleeve. Was thinking of you today. Love always.' Her tattoo can be seen in some scenes throughout the film, including the one inside the mirror when she is wearing a red dress and Colin Farrell is Tony. Ledger himself had a number of tattoos, including the letter 'M' for 'Matilda' on his chest. At a party, when his daughter was 3 months old, he is said to have pointed to the tattoo and declared, 'This is to remind me never to smoke weed again.'

Ledger has been honoured in a number of other ways, too. Indie folk band Bon Iver's song 'Perth' was inspired by him, and rock band Kasabian paid tribute to him in their song 'Vlad the Impaler'. In Perth, the State Theatre Centre of Western Australia named its 575-seat theatre the Heath Ledger Theatre. For its opening, his Oscar for *The Dark Knight* and his Joker costume were on display in the foyer. Ledger didn't live to see the release of *The Dark Knight* but was awarded a plethora of awards posthumously, including the Oscar for Best Supporting Actor, becoming the second actor to win an Academy Award after his death (fellow Australian Peter Finch won Best Actor in a Leading Role for *Network* in 1977 after dying from a heart attack). When Joaquin Phoenix won his cascade of awards in 2020 for his performance in *Joker*, he honoured Ledger in his acceptance speech at the Screen Actors Guild Awards: 'I'm standing here on the shoulders of my favorite actor, Heath Ledger, so thank you and goodnight.'

A couple of months after Ledger passed, rumours emerged that he'd had a secret love child with a married 25-year-old woman in Perth, when he was just 17 years old. The media lapped it up – stating that if this were true, this 'other daughter' could be entitled to part of the star's multimillion-dollar fortune – but the mother of the girl in question refused to confirm if the rumours had any truth in them. When talking about Matilda, Ledger had said, 'I'm born to be a father. And I've been looking forward to this all my life.'

The tragedy of his death didn't just leave the world without his remarkable talent, wondering what he *could* have gone on to achieve, it also left a little girl without her besotted daddy.

Had John Belushi not died, he would have been one of the Ghostbusters.

In *Black Panther*, Chadwick Boseman became the first Black actor to star in a Marvel superhero film.

John Candy played the funnyman – often a big-hearted loser or loudmouthed sidekick with a trademark chuckle – to perfection.

James Dean was the handsome, brooding personification of teenage angst.

Carrie Fisher made a secret cameo in the 1991 *Hook*, alongside *Star Wars* creator George Lucas.

Clark Gable was hailed as 'The King of Hollywood', appearing in more than eighty films throughout his career.

James Gandolfini was awarded the accolade of 'class flirt' in his senior high-school yearbook.

Judy Garland's signature song, 'Over the Rainbow', was almost cut from *The Wizard of Oz* as the sequence was initially thought too long.

At the height of his fame in the 1980s, Corey Haim received 2,000 fan letters a week.

Anne Heche's memorial plaque reads: 'Mother, actress, writer, director, creator, believer. Live in love.'

Philip Seymour Hoffman starred in Hollywood blockbusters, independent films and cult classics such as *The Big Lebowski* and *Boogie Nights*.

© Photograph by PH2 Mark Kettenhofen, Wikimedia Commons

Above: Whitney Houston's 'I Will Always Love You' sat at number one on the Billboard Hot 100 chart for fourteen consecutive weeks in 1992.

Right: The fact that Rock Hudson was gay was an open secret in Hollywood.

Above: Shakespeare's 'Shall I Compare Thee to a Summer's Day?' was read at Heath Ledger's funeral.

Left: Bruce Lee broke down racial barriers in Hollywood, bridging the gap between the East and West in the 1970s.

After starring in the 1972 hardcore porn film *Deep Throat*, Linda Lovelace became the poster girl for the sexual revolution.

© Photograph by CBS Television, Wikimedia Commons

Self-assured, masculine and ruggedly handsome, Steve McQueen earned himself the nickname 'The King of Cool'.

© Photograph by RKO, Wikimedia Commons

Not only a 'blonde bombshell', Marilyn Monroe was also a shrewd businesswoman and civil rights activist.

At the age of 17, Brittany Murphy broke into movies with the now-iconic teen comedy *Clueless*.

Chris Penn had a knack for choosing roles in movies that would become cult classics – like *Reservoir Dogs*, *True Romance* and *Footloose*.

'Don't Give Up' played at Matthew Perry's funeral, which he had said would be the soundtrack to his memoir.

The tragic irony of River Phoenix's passing was described as: 'clean life, dirty death'.

Elvis Presley had many nicknames: The King of Western Bop… The Memphis Flash… The Hillbilly Cat… Elvis the Pelvis…

Kelly Preston fit in making movies around her family life, which she said was her first priority.

Christopher Reeve was never able to 'escape the cape', with audiences always seeing him as Superman, the comic-book hero whose jaw could cut glass.

A man of many talents, Patrick Swayze was a cowboy, gymnast, martial arts expert, singer/songwriter, dancer and, of course, actor.

Sharon Tate's character in *Don't Make Waves* – Malibu – is widely believed to have been the inspiration behind the 1971 Malibu Barbie.

Loving the mystery of the ocean, Paul Walker had intended to pursue marine biology as a career, before acting opportunities sidetracked him.

Robin Williams's big break came in the late 1970s when he played alien Mork in the television sitcom *Mork & Mindy*.

Natalie Wood's career took her from childhood star to teenage ingénue to an alluring starlet who dazzled audiences with her beauty and talent.

Bruce Lee

Age of death: 32

Date of death: 20 July 1973

Cause of death: Cerebral edema (swelling of the brain)

'I am not afraid to die... I will have no regrets, I did what I wanted to do... You can't expect more from life.'

His Life

Have you ever thrown some shapes on the dance floor to the 1974 disco track 'Everybody Was Kung Fu Fighting'? Or kicked butt playing video game *Street Fighter*? Or enjoyed the Marvel movies and comics? If so, you have Bruce Lee to thank. Indeed, with his spirited martial arts moves, the 'fastest fists in the East' was considered responsible for the 1970s kung fu craze; inspiring beat-em-up martial arts video games; and influencing Marvel Comics founder Stan Lee (no relation) to create such characters as Iron Fist and Shang-Chi. Stan Lee considered Bruce to be a superhero without a costume and said that any martial arts character since his death owes their origin to him in one way or another.

Bruce was also responsible for the 'accupunch', which Muhammad Ali used to defeat Richard Dunn in 1975, and which has gone down in history as Ali's final knockout victory. Lee can also take credit for popularizing moves such as the one-inch punch (which Uma Thurman used to escape a coffin after being buried alive in *Kill Bill: Vol. 2*), the straight blast (which an international chain of gyms was named after) and the spinning heel kick (which Lee would pull out in nearly every on-screen fight scene). Despite only weighing around 130 lb to 165 lb (depending on the time of his career), Lee's physical strength was phenomenal. He'd think nothing of doing fifty chin-ups in a row, and push-ups with 125 lb of weight on his back. He inspired the likes of bodybuilders Lou Ferrigno, Lee Haney and Arnold Schwarzenegger.

But it wasn't just his physicality that made Lee stand out from the crowd – he also broke down racial barriers in Hollywood, challenging the Asian stereotype of the emasculated, childlike domestic servant. Lee defied this stereotype to show that Asians can be strong and sexy. As such, he created a new Asian stereotype – the martial artist. At the height of his fame in the 1970s, the movie industry was dominated by white actors, and Lee became a rare non-white movie star, bridging the gap between the East and West, and paving the way for Western martial arts stars like Steven Seagal and Jean-Claude Van Damme.

Lee was always a ball of energy. Born Lee Jun Fan in San Francisco, he grew up in British Hong Kong, and earned a nickname which translates to 'never sits still'. As a teen, he engaged in many street fights, in back alleys and on rooftops, which proved to be an effective training ground for his future vocation. His father was a famous Cantonese opera star, so Lee was introduced to the spotlight from the get-go. Making his first on-screen appearance as a baby in *Golden Gate Girl* in 1941, he went on to appear in many other films as a child, including *The Kid* in 1950, which was his first leading role, starring alongside his father. His Chinese stage name was Lee the Little Dragon, chosen because he was born in both the hour and year of the dragon in the Chinese zodiac. In Chinese culture, the dragon is a symbol of strength, power and good fortune, and is associated with traits such as charisma, ambition and intelligence.

As an adult, Lee lived up to his name, acting/kicking ass in more than twenty movies, his most famous ones being *The Big Boss*, *Fist of Fury*, *Way of the Dragon* (which he also wrote, directed and choreographed the fight scenes for) and *Enter the Dragon*. He starred in the television series *The Green Hornet* and popped up as a guest star in various other shows, including *Batman*, *Blondie* and *Ironside*. During filming, Lee's lightning-fast movements were often so speedy that they couldn't be caught on camera, or made the shot look fake. As such, reshoots were filmed in slow motion so they could be visible to the naked eye, and so his fellow actors could react in a better way; when the initial scenes were played back, Lee's punches were so quick it looked like his combatants simply fell over for no reason. Lee's punching speed was five-hundredths of a second. *Pow!*

Alongside his acting, Lee is credited as the founder of Jeet Kune Do, a hybrid martial arts philosophy that is considered to have laid the groundwork for mixed martial arts (MMA) as we know it today. After moving to Los Angeles, Lee taught martial arts to Chuck Norris, Sharon Tate, James Coburn and Steve McQueen, charging as much as $275 an hour, which equates to around $2,800 today. Lee became personal kung fu instructor to Roman Polanski (Sharon Tate's husband), by which time he was charging nearly $1,000 an hour for lessons. Chuck Norris once said, 'Lee was lightning fast, very agile and incredibly strong for his size.' But Lee wasn't just a tough guy. He was also a poet, an author, a deep thinker and an avid reader who owned around 2,500 books, most of which were based on philosophy. His wife Linda said that he carried a book with him wherever he went. His love of reading and teaching himself new things was such that he dreamed of owning a bookshop before he became a famous martial artist.

Lee met Linda Emery (now Linda Lee Cadwell) while studying at the University of Washington. In many US states, relations between people from different races were banned, so they married in secret in August 1964. They had two children together: Brandon and Shannon, who were just 8 and 4 respectively when their dad died. Brandon became an actor and tragically died himself at the age of 28, when he was accidentally shot by a prop gun on the movie set of *The Crow*. Shannon went on to write the 2020 book entitled *Be Water, My Friend*, taking inspiration from her father's famous advice: 'Empty your mind. Be formless, shapeless, like water... Water can flow or it can crash. Be water, my friend.'

His Death

Bruce Lee's untimely death at the age of 32 was sudden and mysterious. Despite speculation, rumours and conspiracy theories that suggested Lee had been murdered by the Chinese mafia, poisoned by his servant, overdosed on cannabis, died from too much sex, or killed by an ancient curse, it was determined that his cause of death was cerebral edema (swelling of the brain), which occurred after an allergic reaction to the aspirin painkiller Equagesic (which was later discontinued in the US due to its possible toxic side-effects). Since then, some medical professionals have surmised that excessive water consumption or heatstroke may actually have been the true cause of death, particularly considering the fact that Lee had had his sweat glands removed from his armpits as he thought sweat patches looked ugly on screen.

While there are differing accounts as to when the actor was actually declared dead, the 2018 *Bruce Lee: A Life* biography by Matthew Polly – which has been described as 'a definitive account' – states that he died in the bed of his mistress, Taiwanese actress Betty Ting Pei, in Hong Kong, on 20 July 1973. The book states that, complaining of a headache, Lee took Equagesic and went for a nap, missing dinner with film producer Raymond Chow in the process. A while later, unable to rouse Lee, Betty phoned Chow in hysterics. Chow rushed over, to find a sobbing Betty and a lifeless Bruce. It dawned on him that if the news broke that the most famous man in Hong Kong was found dead in his mistress' bed, the press would have a field day. The producer had to orchestrate a scenario where Lee died somewhere else. So he called a doctor, who called an ambulance, which took Lee to Queen Elizabeth Hospital. There, presumably unaware that the patient had been deceased for some time, the medical staff injected drugs into Bruce's heart and applied electric shock treatment. To no avail, obviously. He was pronounced dead.

Six days later, Lee's penultimate movie, *Enter the Dragon*, was released. It went on to become one of the most commercially successful and profitable films of all time, earning more than four times its original budget. The martial arts movie ultimately took $400 million at the worldwide box office, which equates to around $2 billion today. Lee's final movie, *Game of Death*, was released posthumously in 1978. Filming hadn't been completed before he died, so the director, Robert Clouse, finished the movie with a lookalike and archive footage from Lee's other films. The yellow jumpsuit Lee wore in the film has become synonymous with the actor, and fetched $100,500 at auction in 2013. Uma Thurman wears a similar garment in *Kill Bill*.

For a while after Lee's death, a film subgenre known as 'Bruceploitation' exploded onto the scene. Filmmakers from South Korea, Taiwan and Hong Kong would cast Bruce Lee lookalikes (with screen names such as Bruce Li and Bruce Le) to star in imitation martial arts films, with titles such as *Enter Three Dragons* and *New Fist of Fury*. This film trend came to an end in the late 1970s, when Jackie Chan – who began his career as a stunt double and extra in some of Lee's movies – made a name for himself with his kung fu comedies *Drunken Master* and *Snakes in the Eagle's Shadow*.

Actors James Coburn and Steve McQueen were two of the pallbearers at Lee's funeral. He is buried at Lake View Cemetery in Seattle, next to his son Brandon. Bruce's gravestone features an open book with the inscription: 'Your inspiration continues to guide us toward our personal liberation' and a yin and yang symbol, representing harmony. Around 10,000 people visit his grave each year, leaving tokens of their respect such as flowers, messages and incense. Lee is widely celebrated as the most significant martial artist of all time. In 1999, *Time* magazine named him as one of the 100 most influential people of the twentieth century, alongside Muhammad Ali, Marilyn Monroe, Anne Frank, Rosa Parks and Mother Teresa. Whilst many people still theorize and speculate about how Bruce Lee met his end, his widow Linda prefers to look at things differently, saying, 'All these years later, people still wonder about how Bruce died. I prefer to remember how he lived.'

Linda Lovelace

Age of death: 53
Date of death: 22 April 2002
Cause of death: Car accident

'She did things to keep her man happy;
I did things to keep my man from killing me.'

Her Life

'I live for sex… I'm what you might call an exhibitionist.' This is what Linda Lovelace said during her reign as the most well-known porn actress in the world. 'I had been brutalized, raped and forced into every sexual situation imaginable.' This is what she said after she escaped her life as a sex slave. At age 23, Lovelace starred in the 1972 hardcore porn film *Deep Throat*, which became a surprise worldwide phenomenon. It thrust porn into the mainstream – even having a review in *The New York Times* – and made Linda Lovelace a household name. It's been said that the film was produced for around $30,000 and has grossed more than $600 million, making it one of the most financially successful films ever made. Lovelace was paid just $1,250 for her part, which she never saw a penny of.

Born Linda Boreman in The Bronx, New York, her nickname at high school was 'Miss Holy-Holy' as she was known to keep her dates at a distance. Despite having a child at the age of 20 – who she was forced to put up for adoption by her physically abusive mother – Boreman maintained that she was sexually shy and inexperienced. How, then, did this unassuming girl who 'liked to go down by the ocean and hold hands' end up in movies like *Dog Fucker* and *Piss Orgy*, and then go on to become the poster girl for the sexual revolution? Answer: Chuck Traynor. Charming at first, the Jaguar-driving photographer and bar owner soon grew violent, abusive and terrifying. He became Linda's husband and pimp, frequently beating her, forcing her to have sex with men for money, and threatening to kill her and her family if she complained or tried to escape. Linda became his prisoner, where he slept on top of her at night and listened to her phone calls with a gun pointed to her head. Of her first experience of prostitution – a gang rape by five men – Linda said that she'd never been so terrified, degraded and humiliated in all her life. 'I felt like garbage.'

Had *Deep Throat* moviegoers – who included Frank Sinatra, Truman Capote, Shirley MacLaine, Jack Nicholson and Hugh Hefner – known of the abuse its star was having to endure, perhaps they'd have opted to watch *The Godfather* (another of the year's top movies) instead. Hefner invited Lovelace and Traynor to his Playboy Mansion, where they rubbed shoulders (and other things) with Hollywood stars. Rat-Packer Sammy Davis Jr. was so taken with Lovelace that they began a relationship of sorts, which involved group sex with their spouses. Still under Traynor's control, in 1974, Lovelace went on to make *Deep Throat II* and publish two memoirs, *Inside Linda Lovelace* and *The Intimate Diary of Linda Lovelace*. She also posed for *Playboy*, *Esquire* and *Bachelor*. Before interviews, Traynor would tell her what to say – that she loved sex, couldn't get enough, etc. – threatening to beat/kill her if she went off-script.

When Linda began rehearsing for a musical stage show, she developed a newfound confidence, perhaps because the people she was working with treated her as a human being, rather than a piece of meat. While her previous attempts to escape from Traynor had led to severe beatings, humiliations and death threats, after two years of marriage, Linda plucked up the courage to leave for good. She had to hide out in hotels and disguises for weeks until Traynor finally accepted that she wasn't going back to him. In her 1980 autobiography *Ordeal*, she revealed the horrors she endured and asserted that her previous two books – which were pro-porn – were filled with lies, concocted by Traynor.

In 1975, Linda began dating producer, choreographer and *West Side Story* actor David Winters. He produced the comedy sex farce *Linda Lovelace for President*, which saw the actress on a campaign trail following a bus route mapped out in the shape of a penis, and the audience rolling its collective eyes to lines like 'At least she knows how to use her head'. The following year, she was cast to play the lead role in erotic film *Forever Emmanuelle* (also known as *Laure*) but then stated that God had changed her life and refused to do any nudity – even objecting to the Venus de Milo statue on set due to its bare breasts. It's reported that she was taking large quantities of cocaine and amphetamines at the time. The part was given instead to French actress Annie Belle.

In 1976, Linda married Larry Marchiano, who was about as far removed from show business as could be: he was a cable installer and later owned a drywall business. The couple had two children, but divorced after twenty-two years of marriage, remaining on good terms. Linda became a grandmother in 1998, and worked day and night in low-paying jobs to make ends meet.

Linda's fourth book, *Out of Bondage*, focused on her life after she'd left Traynor. But escaping her past life didn't mean that things were suddenly easy. During a double mastectomy, necessary due to complications from the silicone implants Traynor had forced her to have, it was found that Linda's liver was on the verge of collapse (she had contracted hepatitis C from a blood transfusion after she'd been in a serious car accident back in 1970). As a result, she had to undergo a liver transplant. As well as becoming a born-again Christian, Linda became a spokeswoman for the anti-pornography movement, speaking at colleges, before feminist groups and at government hearings. The unlikely feminist icon testified before the Attorney General's Commission on pornography, also called the Meese Report, asserting that whoever watches *Deep Throat* is witnessing her being raped. She called it a 'crime' that the movie was still being showed, saying, 'There was a gun to my head the entire time.'

Her Death

On 3 April 2002, whilst driving to hospital for kidney dialysis, Linda was involved in a serious road accident, which saw her being thrown from her SUV. She sustained severe injuries and was put on life-support at Denver Health Medical Center. On 22 April – with Larry Marchiano and their two children by her side – this was switched off. Linda was 53 years old. She was cremated and her ashes buried in an unmarked grave next to her in-laws – Larry's parents – at Parker Cemetery. The plot was originally intended for Larry himself but he gave it to Linda following her death. It was her family's wish to leave the grave unmarked for fear that it would be a target for vandalism due to Linda's past.

Indeed, since her death – as with during her life – Linda has not always been shown the respect she deserves. As illustrated by country singer David Allan Coe's song 'I Made Linda Lovelace Gag', and the 'I choked Linda Lovelace' T-shirts doing the rounds on Etsy and similar websites. But the 2013 biopic *Lovelace*, starring Amanda Seyfried, showed a more rounded depiction of the star behind the world's most famous blue movie, including the abuse she suffered at the hands of Traynor. Linda's son, Dominic Marchiano, praised the film, pleased that his mother was being shown in a new light. 'I am proud of my mom and hope [the film] will create a new awareness on the subject matter,' he said. 'She was a survivor… and a wonderful person.' Feminist lawyer Catharine A. MacKinnon, who had campaigned with Linda to ban porn films, described her as 'sweet, strong, smart and real'.

Theatre productions were also created about Linda, such as the 2008 *Lovelace: A Rock Musical* and the 2010 *The Deep Throat Sex Scandal*. The X-rated *Deep Throat* has remained fascinating to audiences, and the 2005 documentary *Inside Deep Throat* – narrated by Dennis Hopper – explored Linda's participation in the movie. The trailer describes it as 'the film that was made for next to nothing, but changed everything'.

Steve McQueen

Age of death: 50

Date of death: 7 November 1980

Cause of death: Cardiac arrest, following cancer surgery

'I live for myself and I answer to nobody.'

His Life

Call it fate, call it luck, call it a higher power… Call it what you will but something was working in Steve McQueen's favour the night of 9 August 1969. Indeed, at the age of 39, the actor dodged a gruesome death. He was supposed to be a guest at Sharon Tate's house the night that she – and everyone else present – was brutally murdered by the 'Manson Family'. McQueen unwittingly escaped the horror by instead choosing to spend the night with a 'beautiful blonde'. Chillingly, after Manson was apprehended by police, a hit list was discovered of Hollywood celebrities who he planned to kill – with McQueen, Elizabeth Taylor, Richard Burton and Frank Sinatra among his targets. Freaked out by this close call, McQueen tightened up the security measures at his home and began carrying a loaded Magnum pistol at all times.

Thank goodness 'The King of Cool' was blessed with over a decade more on this planet. Had he not been, we'd never have seen him make Hollywood history in 1974, when he became the highest paid actor in the world, for his role in *The Towering Inferno*. We'd also never have seen him nominated for two Golden Globes – one in 1970 for Best Actor in a Comedy or Musical for his role in *The Reivers*, and one in 1974 for Best Actor in a Drama for *Papillon*. Or seen him light up the screen with his ruggedly handsome good looks, masculine self-assurance and anti-hero aloofness in the nine other films he appeared in between 1970 and 1980, including *Le Mans*, *The Getaway* and *An Enemy of the People*. Prior to this, some of his hit movies included: *The Blob, The Magnificent Seven*, *The Great Escape*, *The Cincinnati Kid*, *The Sand Pebbles* (for which he was nominated for an Oscar as Best Actor in a Leading Role) and *The Thomas Crown Affair*. He didn't just star in films that started with 'The', however, as proved with *Soldier in the Rain*, *Tom Horn* and *Bullitt*. He could have starred in a handful of movies that went on to become classics, like *Apocalypse Now, Butch Cassidy and the Sundance Kid, Dirty Harry, Breakfast at Tiffany's, The French Connection* and *One Flew Over The Cuckoo's Nest,* but turned the roles in these films down.

The action thriller *Bullitt* allowed McQueen to stoke one of his passions: driving fast. He considered being a professional race car driver but ultimately chose acting – able to get his fix from fast-paced scenes in some of his movies. He once said, 'I'm not sure whether I'm an actor who races or a racer who acts.' In *Bullitt* – during the legendary car-chase scene up and down the hills of San Francisco that has been endlessly imitated since – he was at the wheel during all of the close-ups shots, with a stuntman filming the more tricky manoeuvres. McQueen also performed some of his own stunts during the motorcycle-chase scene in *The Great Escape*. At one point, with the use of editing, McQueen is seen wearing a German uniform and chasing himself on a different bike. In real life, he owned around 100 classic motorcycles and about 100 other vehicles, including trucks, vans, Jeeps, buggies, and luxury and vintage cars, including Porsches, Ferraris and Jaguars.

Just as he wasn't faithful to one mode of transport, McQueen also wasn't faithful to one woman. He was married three times – to actress and dancer Neile Adams (with whom he had two children, Chad – who played Dutch in 1984's *The Karate Kid* – and Terry, who sadly died from respiratory failure aged 38), actress Ali MacGraw (his co-star in *The Getaway*) and model Barbara Minty (who was twenty-four years his junior). Whilst married, he was very open about the fact that he wouldn't curb his womanizing ways and would often flaunt the affairs he'd had with co-stars, aspiring actresses who he'd 'interview' in his hotel suite at the Beverly Wilshire, starstruck fans, prostitutes… and the previously mentioned 'beautiful blonde'. His friend Cliff Coleman recalled a time when they were driving along a motorway in England together in a rental car. McQueen saw a pretty girl in the next lane and waved at her; she waved back. Without a word, the lothario pulled over, and so did she. 'He calmly got in her car and that was the last we saw of him for two days.' Another time when McQueen's rampant carnal desires were displayed was during the filming of *The Magnificent Seven*; he and co-star Robert Vaughn spent Good Friday in a Mexican brothel, getting drunk on margaritas and toasting the movie's title by sharing seven prostitutes between them.

Unloved by his alcoholic prostitute mother, abandoned by his circus stuntman father and beaten by his two stepfathers, the actor's childhood was an unhappy one: 'I come from the gutter,' he once said. His debauched lifestyle began young, losing his virginity to a teenage prostitute, who accepted cakes as payment, at the age of 13. By 16, he was working as a towel boy in a brothel. He turned to petty crime, shoplifting, stealing hubcaps and such, and wound up in the California Junior Boys Republic Reformatory School. McQueen kept a lifelong association with the institution and, when he was working on films, would request that the studios give him items such as jeans and electric razors, which he would then donate to the boys residing there. He would also visit to spend time with the students, talking about his experiences and playing pool with them. After leaving the school, McQueen enlisted in the United States Marine Corps at age 17, which he said 'made a man out of [him]'. Then, following stints as a getaway driver for bank robbers, a pimp, and a seller of illegal handguns, McQueen decided to turn his life around with acting. Although he became one of Hollywood's hottest stars, he remained no angel. In 1972, he was arrested for drink-driving, and was well acquainted with illegal substances, including cocaine, marijuana, LSD and other hallucinogens.

In 1979, McQueen was diagnosed with pleural mesothelioma, a cancer associated with asbestos exposure, which he probably first came into contact with whilst serving in the Marines, then when wearing the flame-retardant racing suits. At first, he publicly denied he had cancer to spare his family and friends pain and to retain his dignity. He travelled to Mexico to seek unconventional treatments, which included coffee enemas, daily injections of fluid containing cells from sheep and cattle, psychotherapy and prayer sessions. After word got out that McQueen was sick and seeking such treatment, traditional cancer organizations were alarmed, with one doctor calling the therapy 'rank quackery'. McQueen issued a statement saying, 'Mexico is showing the world a new way of fighting cancer through nonspecific metabolic therapies,' adding, 'Thank you for helping to save my life.'

His Death

On 7 November 1980, in the early hours of the morning – around thirteen hours after surgery to remove numerous tumours in his abdomen and neck – Steve McQueen suffered a heart attack and died, at age 50. He was at Clínica Santa Rosa in Juárez, Mexico, and had checked in under the pseudonym Samuel Sheppard. His surgeon, Dr Cesar Santos Vargas (who had earned a medical reputation years earlier for treating injured bullfighters), described his patient as 'a man sure of himself and very sincere'. He added that, after the operation, McQueen 'had a desire to live when he knew the race [against death] was at a short distance'. Two family friends were at his bedside when he died, with his two children and wife Barbara having just left the clinic. His final words were in Spanish – 'Lo hice', which means 'I did it'.

McQueen's body was transported to El Paso International Airport and flown to LA via private jet. The casket was placed on the plane by three of the actor's friends. Seeing *Times* photographer Carlos Rosales, who had been tasked with covering the story, they crowded around him, forcibly took his camera and removed its roll of film. One of the men told him: 'If Steve McQueen had been alive today, he would have punched you out. He punched out people like you.' At McQueen's request, there was no funeral or memorial service. The family asked that donations be made to the California Junior Boys Republic Reformatory School. He was cremated and his ashes were scattered in the Pacific Ocean.

Posthumously, McQueen was awarded many honours, including a star on the Hollywood Walk of Fame in 1986, an induction into the Motorcycle Hall of Fame in 1999, and an induction into the Hall of Great Western Performers in 2007. Countless books have been written about him, including the tell-all memoir *My Husband, My Friend* by his first wife. In it, Neile recounts their rollercoaster fifteen-and-a-half-year marriage, revealing 'his good side, his crazy side, his dark side'. She wrote that his jealousy and paranoia once saw him beating her, and holding a gun to her head, demanding to know who she'd had a fling with.

Between 2007 and 2016, McQueen was amongst the top twelve highest-earning dead celebrities, with his estate raking in between $6 million and $9 million a year. Thanks to lucrative licensing deals with various brands, the money keeps rolling in. Fans could dress head to toe in McQueen merch if they so desired, with Persol sunglasses; Barbour T-shirts, jumpers, jackets and trousers; Playboy chukka boots; and the Tag Heuer Monaco Chronograph watch that the actor famously sported in the film *Le Mans* to finish off the ensemble. Or simply pull on a pair of 'Steve McQueens' ('jeans' in Cockney rhyming slang). Much memorabilia – cars, motorcycles, watches, sunglasses – driven/worn by the star has been auctioned off for millions of dollars. The Ford Mustang driven by McQueen in *Bullitt* sold for a record $3.74 million in 2020. Ford acquired the rights to use McQueen's image in its advertising campaigns, producing various television ads for its cars: the 1998 Ford Puma, the 2005 Ford Mustang and the 2019 Mustang Bullitt, with McQueen's granddaughter – actress Molly McQueen – starring in the latter. Different taglines were used in all of the commercials, but perhaps the most apt was the one in the 'Field of Dreams' Ford Mustang ad, which sees McQueen stepping out of a cornfield to take the car for a spin around a winding racetrack: 'The Legend Lives'.

Marilyn Monroe

Age of death: 36

Date of death: 4 August 1962

Cause of death: Drug overdose

*'We should all start to live before we get too old.
Fear is stupid. So are regrets.'*

Her Life

Marilyn Monroe was luminous, effervescent, dazzling… and hopelessly unhappy. Behind the radiant smiles, hip-swinging walks and suggestive comments (like 'It's not true I had nothing on, I had the radio on') was a sad, lonely woman, trying desperately to escape the trauma of her childhood. With an absent father and a mentally unwell mother, she endured an existence in and out of foster homes and an orphanage, being subjected to sexual abuse along the way. At the age of 16, she married her nextdoor neighbour, 21-year-old James Dougherty – but the union only lasted four years. This was considerably longer than Marilyn's second marriage – to baseball star Joe DiMaggio – which lasted nine months, with Marilyn citing 'mental cruelty' on the divorce papers. The blonde bombshell's third marriage, to playwright Arthur Miller, was equally doomed, ending after five years – during which time Marilyn reportedly suffered two miscarriages and one ectopic pregnancy. When she married Miller, Monroe converted to Judaism, which led to all of her films being banned in Egypt.

While the star may not have had much success in her love life, on screen it was a different story. Beginning her career as a pin-up model, she changed her name from Norma Jeane Baker to Marilyn Monroe ('Marilyn' after Broadway star Marilyn Miller and 'Monroe' as it was her mother's maiden name) and started seeking the attention of film studio executives. And attention she got! The year 1953 was a big one for Marilyn, as she starred in three top-billing films – *Niagara*, *Gentlemen Prefer Blondes* and *How to Marry a Millionaire* – and appeared in *Playboy*'s first edition, both on the front cover and as the centrefold. While she hadn't consented to being featured (the nude photos had been taken previously when she was hard up for cash), it didn't hurt her career – as her bosses had feared it would – but instead boosted her popularity (fancy that). Although founder of *Playboy* Hugh Hefner never met the woman who helped to make him famous, he is spending forever with her, having bought the crypt next to hers. 'Spending eternity next to Marilyn is too sweet to pass up,' he'd said years before his death in 2017, after he'd purchased the plot.

Between 1947 and 1961, Marilyn was in more than thirty movies – including *Some Like It Hot*, *All About Eve* and *The Asphalt Jungle* – singing, dancing, acting and titillating audiences the world over. In a bid to 'fight' the studio system and make movies that she wanted to, she set up a production company – Marilyn Monroe Productions (MMP) – which produced *The Prince and the Showgirl*. *Time* called her a 'shrewd businesswoman' – a far cry from the dim-witted sex symbol that had become her typecast persona. Not only shrewd, Monroe was also highly principled and strived for social justice. A great friend of Ella Fitzgerald, Marilyn fought for civil rights in the 1950s when LA nightclub Mocambo refused to hire Ella because she was Black. The high-profile actress told the owner that she would sit in the front row every night that Fitzgerald sang if he booked her. She kept her word, which brought a huge amount of publicity and boosted the jazz singer's career. Ella said that she never had to play a small jazz club again, and described Marilyn as 'an unusual woman – a little ahead of her times. And she didn't know it'.

Marilyn's personal life was never dull. She embarked on affairs with the two Kennedy brothers – John F. Kennedy and Attorney General Robert Kennedy. She may have gotten pregnant by one of them, then had an abortion. Due to her dalliances with men in such high power, and her previous marriage to suspected communist sympathizer Arthur Miller, the FBI took an interest in Monroe. Her house was bugged, her phones tapped, and reports were produced on her alleged links to the communist party and her potential knowledge of nuclear government secrets, as disclosed by the Kennedys. It was feared that this 'dumb blonde' was a threat to national security.

Marilyn was plagued with mental-health issues throughout her short life – at times undergoing treatment at psychiatric clinics. Experts have said that if she were around today, she may have been diagnosed with borderline personality disorder, due to symptoms such as: a confused identity, unstable relationships, extreme emotional volatility, impulsivity and addictive behaviour, as displayed by her addiction to barbiturates (sleeping pills), amphetamines and alcohol (particularly Dom Perignon champagne). Monroe became notorious on-set for holding up filming, with her tardiness, demands for dozens of retakes and fluffing of lines. Even when she was creating movie magic, she suffered from terrible stage fright, low self-esteem and neuroses. 'Spectacular absenteeism' and 'unprofessional antics' got her fired from the set of *Something's Got to Give*. Fox Studios filed a $750,000 lawsuit against her, but later agreed to take her back after co-star Dean Martin refused to work on the film with any other actress. Alas, the picture was never completed due to Monroe's death. Her last film to be released was *The Misfits*, which was also Clark Gable's final movie before his untimely death. Despite the frustrations the starlet caused while filming her movies, director Billy Wilder (who was so angry with her that she wasn't invited to the wrap party of *Some Like It Hot*) conceded: 'For what you finally got on screen, she was worth every hour you had to wait for her… How often do you have a face like hers that lights up a screen?'

Her Death

On 4 August 1962, after seeing the light on under Marilyn's locked bedroom door at around 3 am, her housekeeper called the star's psychiatrist Dr Ralph Greenson, worried that something was wrong. He gained entry into the bedroom by smashing a window and found his patient lying face down, naked, on the bed, with her hand clutching the phone and an empty bottle of sleeping pills beside her, plus fourteen other pill bottles on the bedside table. Monroe was 36 years old. Given the amount of barbiturates in her system and the fact that no foul play was detected, Marilyn's death was ruled a 'probable suicide' – not an accidental overdose. It wasn't until later that theories of foul play began to circulate. It came to light that Robert Kennedy had paid his mistress a visit on that fateful day. They had argued, with Bobby yelling at her, telling the distraught star that their relationship was over. Some people (including her friend Frank Sinatra) believe Marilyn was murdered – perhaps so she never got the chance to go public about her clandestine affairs with the Kennedys, or to avoid government secrets being revealed – and the crime covered up by those in power. George Cukor, who had directed Marilyn in *Let's Make Love* and *Something's Got to Give*, described her death as 'a nasty business', saying, 'Her worst rejection. Power and money. In the end she was too innocent.' Whatever the circumstances of her demise, no one denies that Marilyn was in a fragile state on the day of her death. She had made many phone calls, including one to Peter Lawford, brother-in-law to the Kennedys. Calling to cancel a dinner invitation as she didn't feel well, she had said: 'Will you say goodbye to Pat [Lawford's wife] and to Jack [the President] and to yourself, because you're a nice guy?'

In her bedroom, a half-written love note to her second husband Joe DiMaggio was found. Despite having been divorced for eight years, they had remained friends and he helped to arrange her funeral, along with Marilyn's business manager Inez Melson and half-sister Berniece Baker Miracle. The service was held at LA's Westwood Village Memorial Park Cemetery, attended by just thirty-one close family and friends, with hundreds of mourners crowding the streets around the cemetery. Marilyn was buried in her favourite outfit – a pale green Pucci dress with matching chiffon scarf. For the next two decades, DiMaggio sent red roses several times a week to his ex-wife's grave. On his own death bed, at the age of 84 in 1999, he'd said: 'I'll finally get to see Marilyn.' Monroe's crypt is located in the cemetery's Corridor of Memories (number 24) and is often marked by the lipstick kisses of her fans.

Although Monroe's impact on the world throughout her life was remarkable, it is perhaps even greater in death. Her legend has endured for way more than half a century – and shows no sign of slipping away. Many films have been made about her life, including *Blonde*; *Love, Marilyn;* and *My Week with Marilyn*, for which Michelle Williams scooped a Golden Globe and was nominated for an Oscar in 2012 for her portrayal of the damaged diva. *The Seven Year Itch* (1955) features one of the most iconic scenes in the history of film, in which Monroe stands above a subway grate in a white dress and allows it to blow up, exposing her legs. The dress sold at auction for $4.6 million in 2011 and the scene has been aped in countless films, including *The Woman in Red*, *The Smurfs*, *Kingpin* and *Shrek 2*. Another of Marilyn's most memorable garments – the skin-tight dress adorned with 6,000 hand-sewn crystals she wore to sing 'Happy Birthday, Mr President' to John F. Kennedy at his forty-fifth birthday celebrations – sold for $4.8 million in 2016. It was famously worn by Kim Kardashian for the 2022 Met Gala, causing much controversy.

Everyone from David Bowie to Beyoncé, Keith Urban to Metallica has referenced Monroe in their songs – with Madonna's 'Material Girl' video recreating the 'Diamonds are a Girl's Best Friend' scene from *Gentlemen Prefer Blondes*. Elton John wrote 'Candle in the Wind' in 1973 in memory of Monroe; the song was rewritten in 1997 after the death of Princess Diana. Marilyn's sex appeal is matched only by her 'spend appeal', with her name and image having been licensed for hundreds of products by more than seventy-five brands in their ad campaigns – from Chanel No. 5 to Coca-Cola, Sony to Snickers. She has also inspired TV shows, art, fashion, architecture, literature, graphic novels, poetry, opera, theatre, video games… and a rice field in Japan containing a 140- by 100-metre image of Monroe made from nine species of rice.

According to *The Guide to United States Popular Culture*, 'no other star has ever inspired such a wide range of emotions – from lust to pity, from envy to remorse'. She was a one-off, a true icon. She had more to give, but never got the chance. Indeed, her candle burned out long before her legend ever did.

Brittany Murphy

Age of death: 32

Date of death: 20 December 2009

Cause of death: Pneumonia

'I would like to be very, very, very, very old. With all the technology we are inventing and what they are coming up with scientifically, people are having longer lifetimes.'

Her Life

'Huggable, but not fuckable' was what Brittany Murphy was told she was by a top movie executive. And she was deemed 'the fat, ugly chick [from *Clueless*]' by radio host Howard Stern. Nice. The movie executive told Murphy that if she wanted to be leading-lady material, she'd need to address this issue. And address it she did. Her curly dark hair? Gone, and replaced with blonde, straight hair extensions. Her healthy-looking figure? Diminished to 115 lb, most likely at the hands (or fingers) of an eating disorder. Her sense of self? Seemingly on hiatus. But her extreme makeover did the trick. By around the age of 25, she was now 'fuckable', and was cast in various movies – such as *Just Married*, *Little Black Book*, *Uptown Girls* and *Love (and Other Disasters)* – as the leading lady. While this may have pleased the unnamed top movie executive, audiences were left short-changed and critics unimpressed (the above movies scoring a paltry twenty per cent, twenty-two per cent, thirteen per cent and twenty per cent respectively on review website Rotten Tomatoes).

Previously, Murphy had been cast in grittier, more complex roles in movies a million miles from these lighthearted comedies. She played troubled psychiatric patients very well, as seen with her characters in *Freeway*, *Don't Say a Word* and *Girl, Interrupted*. For the latter, she was nominated in the Young Artists Awards for Best Young Lead Actress in a Feature Film. Some – including her friend and co-star in *King of the Hill* Kathy Najimy – say she should have won an Oscar for her performance. Voicing the character of Luanne Platter in *King of the Hill* saw Murphy taking home the accolade for Best Voice Acting in an Animated Television Production in the 2005 Annie Awards, which recognize excellence in the world of animation. She worked on the show from its very beginning in 1997 until her death in 2009. Brittany was also the voice of the feisty, flirty penguin Gloria in *Happy Feet*, where she sang two of the film's songs – Queen's 'Somebody to Love' and Earth, Wind & Fire's 'Boogie Wonderland'. She had a beautiful singing voice, also performing Carly Simon's 'Nobody Does it Better' in *Little Black Book* and dance tune 'Faster Kill Pussycat' by DJ Paul Oakenfold, who described her as 'cool' and 'unique', with a strong, powerful voice. 'Her voice is great on the record, I think people will be surprised when they hear it,' he'd said. The song reached number one on the US Billboard Hot Dance Club Play Chart, and number seven on the UK Singles Chart.

Before all of this, in 1995, at the age of 17, Murphy got her big break into movies with the now-iconic teen comedy *Clueless*. Cast as Tai, the 'misfit who gets a makeover', she nailed the audition, with co-star Alicia Silverstone recalling that when Murphy walked out of the room, she exclaimed: 'You guys! Did you see that?' And see that they did. Despite appearing in many popular TV shows of the 1990s – *Blossom*, *Frasier*, *Party of Five, Boy Meets World* and *Sister, Sister* – *Clueless* was the launch of the star's successful career. She went from full-on kooky (*Cherry Falls, Riding in Cars With Boys*) to kinda kooky *and* sexy (*8 Mile*, *Sin City*), following her real-life makeover. Despite her success, Murphy was plagued by insecurity. Hardly surprising, given the comments of the aforementioned movie executive et al. Her self-deprecating comments about her appearance ('I look at old photos of the premiere of *Clueless* and I look like a meatball on top of another meatball') were cute to a point, but they only served to highlight the fact that in the image-obsessed world of Hollywood, Murphy felt she was never good enough.

Perhaps this self-doubt led Murphy into the arms of British screenwriter Simon Monjack. Charming and charismatic at first, he showered the actress with attention… and lies. Amongst his tall tales were that he had a collection of seventeen Ferraris, had dated Elle McPherson and Madonna, was the biggest Johannes Vermeer collector, had been dying of terminal brain cancer so had bought an experimental treatment from the fins of sharks which saved his life, and was a billionaire. In fact, he owed a lot of people money and allegedly went through $3 million of Brittany's cash in three years, saying he was investing it in jewellery, property, real estate, and stocks and bonds. But much of the money was used to put one of his two children (who Brittany knew nothing of) through private school in the UK. Many described Simon as a controlling narcissist; it wasn't long before Brittany fired her agent, manager, lawyer and other people around her – and he became all of these things. He even became her make-up artist! Trista Jordan, the actual make-up artist on Brittany's last film, *Something Wicked*, wasn't impressed: 'Simon had taken a red tube of lipstick and drawn lips outside her natural lip line like a clown. Her blush was lopsided.' Kathy Najimy looks back now, saying that Simon had come along during a time in Brittany's life when she was having 'a little dip' and that she became 'prey'. The couple married in April 2007. People were unable to contact Murphy directly; she had no access to her email account or phone, and everything went through Simon. Concerned friends say Murphy became unrecognizable – too thin, spaced out, sad – and they attempted an intervention. It failed, with both Brittany and her mother Sharon (who lived with the couple) declaring, 'We love Simon and we believe Simon.'

Her Death

Although the cause of Brittany Murphy's death was officially recorded as pneumonia – with secondary factors of severe anaemia and drug intoxication from over-the-counter and prescription medications – her passing still remains a mystery. She died on 20 December 2009, at the age of 32, having collapsed in her bathroom and going into cardiac arrest. She was transported to Cedars-Sinai Medical Center but attempts to resuscitate her were in vain. Four days later, on Christmas Eve, the actress was buried at Forest Lawn Memorial Park in the Hollywood Hills, with a small service held for close family and friends, officiated by both a Christian minister and a rabbi. 'Amazing Grace' was sung at her gravesite by those in attendance, and the ceremony ended with a reading from one of her favourite books, *The Little Prince* by Antoine de Saint-Exupéry. Simon spoke at the service, saying that the 'closeness and beauty of [their] love will live on forever'.

In the time following Brittany's death, Simon and Sharon's behaviour was what can only be described as 'odd'. The interview they gave together on chat show *Larry King Live* made for uncomfortable viewing, as did the strange mother and son-in-law photo shoot they did, which saw them hugging each other and looking forlorn. In the midst of their grief, they would climb into bed together and cry. Their behaviour roused suspicion and fuelled many theories about Brittany's death.

In a bizarre turn of events, Simon died five months after Brittany did, on 23 May 2010, also from pneumonia and anaemia. The Los Angeles County Department of Health considered that the couple's house could have contained toxic mould, which led to their deaths, but this was dismissed by Los Angeles Assistant Chief Coroner Ed Winter, who said there were 'no indicators' that mould was a factor. (Winter was known as the 'Coroner to the Stars', having handled investigations into the deaths of celebrities such as Michael Jackson, Whitney Houston, Tom Petty, Corey Haim and Paul Walker.)

Murphy's father, Angelo Bertolotti, didn't believe that pneumonia was the cause of his daughter's death and suspected foul play, even accusing Brittany's mother (who he left when Brittany was 1 year old; he wasn't involved in raising her) of killing her and Monjack so she could inherit their estate. He said on *Good Morning America,* 'I have a feeling that there was a definite murder situation here.' Bertolotti hired a private toxicologist, who tested samples of Brittany's hair and found high levels of heavy metals in it, including barium, which is used in some rat poisons. But heavy metals weren't found in her bloodstream and experts determined that the metals in her hair most likely came from hairspray and hair dye.

Outraged at the accusation, Sharon wrote an open letter, published in *The Hollywood Reporter* in 2013, stating, 'The lab Angelo used, if you can call it that, is an internet site that farmed out the actual testing and then wrote horribly untrue things under the guise of "analysis".' She wrote that Angelo's accusations were self-serving and that he only wanted to trade on Brittany's life, career and good reputation 'at the cost of putting a cloud over her memory'. Sharon has stayed out of the limelight since writing this letter and didn't appear in the 2021 two-part documentary *What Happened, Brittany Murphy?*, despite the director tracking her down via a private investigator and hand-delivering a note asking her to be involved.

In the documentary, amongst the theories, analysis and unanswered questions surrounding Brittany's death are video clips of the young, excitable actress, and interviews of people who worked with her and loved her. Kathy Najimy described her as '*so* wonderful', and that there was 'nobody else like her', while her *8 Mile* co-star Taryn Manning remembered her as 'free-spirited, whimsical and full of laughter… like a butterfly that you can't catch'.

Other tributes from stars are similarly complimentary. On Twitter (now X), Jessica Simpson described the actress as 'an incredible ray of light' and said that 'her smile was contagious'; Lindsay Lohan said she had a 'beautiful soul'; and Murphy's ex-boyfriend and co-star in *Just Married*, Ashton Kutcher, tweeted after her death: '2day the world lost a little piece of sunshine,' adding, 'see you on the other side, kid.' In an Instagram post, Alyssa Milano likened Murphy to 'a magical unicorn', saying, 'It brought her joy to bring joy to others.'

Chris Penn

Age of death: 40

Date of death: 24 January 2006

Cause of death: Heart disease

'More power to the people who get to choose their roles. I don't.'

His Life

'I just want to introduce myself. Rick Stifler. The Big Stiff. Stevie's dad.' These are words uttered by a character played by Chris Penn that never came to pass. Whilst cast as Stifler's dad in the 2001 *American Pie 2*, the character was ultimately cut from the movie as test audiences weren't interested in seeing that the apple hadn't fallen far from the tree, which explained why the foul-mouthed, sex-obsessed Steve Stifler was the way he was. Penn described the character as 'an asshole who never grew up'.

A much more well-known 'asshole' who Penn played was Nice Guy Eddie, son of the gangster mastermind in the 1992 *Reservoir Dogs*. It was one of his most memorable roles, but he almost never got to play it. Before the film's budget was increased, the role of Nice Guy Eddie was earmarked for producer Lawrence Bender (who ended up playing a cop).

Penn had a knack for choosing roles in movies that would become cult classics – as well as *Reservoir Dogs*, there was the 1993 *True Romance*, in which he played vengeful detective Nicky Dimes, and the more lighthearted *Footloose* (1984), which saw him dancing up a storm in dungarees, alongside Kevin Bacon. Then there were the less notable roles: a lying, drunk guy in *Josh and S.A.M.*, a marijuana-dealing janitor in *Murder by Numbers*, the hapless dog-napping crook in *Beethoven's 2nd*…

More a character actor than a leading man, Penn was irked by this classification, stating: 'Everybody says "Chris, you're a great character actor". I mean, my whole career. Why? Because I'm fat?… How about just I'm a good actor?' At more than 300 lb at the time of his death, Penn's demise was attributed to his weight by his older brother, actor Sean Penn. During an interview with Larry King, Sean said that his brother had been 'a fantastically self-abusing guy over periods of his life' but that this wasn't the case in the end. He added: 'It was a natural death. But a natural death that was brought on by some hard living, but particularly weight.'

One period of Chris's life when he 'fantastically self-abused' was after the death of his 2-day-old daughter. He admitted he used his grief as an excuse to do as many drugs as possible. It took him about a year to realize what he was doing and, by that point, he was addicted. During his five-year cocaine addiction, Penn got arrested for bar brawls and became notorious for his wild behaviour. Michael Madsen – who co-starred with him in *Reservoir Dogs*, *Mulholland Falls*, *The Florentine* and *Papertrail* – recalled one crazy night when the pair broke into a bar/liquor store through the roof and, realizing they couldn't get out through the door, had to construct a tower of chairs on the bar in order to climb back out. He described his friend as a 'wonderful, wonderful guy' and a 'tough son of a gun'. *Slant* magazine characterized Penn as 'a human hand grenade who lived to pull his own pin'. Elaborating with: 'He was a nasty daredevil, fearless and playful and game for anything.'

Embarking on his acting career at the age of 12 at Loft Studio, it would appear that Chris lived most of his life in the shadow of his multi-award-winning brother Sean, who has been catapulted into 'superstar' territory. But despite the sibling rivalry that one might imagine, the two were close. They also have another sibling, musician Michael Penn. Chris and Sean appeared as brothers in the 1986 family drama *At Close Range*, alongside their mother, Eileen Ryan (who played various characters throughout her six-decade career, including the long-suffering matriarch Marilyn in the 1989 *Parenthood*). The arts clearly ran through the family's blood, with their father, Leo Penn, an accomplished TV-series director.

Chris and Sean were high-school friends with Emilio Estevez, Charlie Sheen, Rob Lowe and Chad Lowe, who would all make short films together. *At Close Range* also starred Christopher Walken, who appeared in two other movies with Chris: *True Romance* and *The Funeral*. The latter saw Penn winning the award for Best Supporting Actor at the Venice Film Festival in 1996. He played Chez, an unhinged gangster seeking revenge for the death of his brother. (Another accolade came in the form of a shared Golden Globe for the 1993 *Short Cuts*.)

Penn seemed comfortable playing violent criminals with a bad temper, in films such as *Rush Hour*, *Stealing Harvard*, *Corky Romano* and, of course,

Reservoir Dogs. On the flipside, he also has a number of law-enforcement roles under his belt: in *Mulholland Falls*, *Liar*, *Papertrail*, *Starsky & Hutch*, *King of Sorrow*, *True Romance* and *To Wong Foo, Thanks for Everything! Julie Newmar*. He also appeared on the small screen, in television shows such as *Seinfeld*, *Will & Grace*, *CSI: Miami*, *Law & Order: Criminal Intent* and *Entourage*, and was the voice of Officer Eddie Pulaski in computer game *Grand Theft Auto*.

The Independent called Penn 'one of Hollywood's most perplexing actors'. He could play tough, he could play goofy, he could play crazed, he could play vulnerable… He delivered his lines with heart and authenticity, once saying: 'When I act, I don't even know there's a camera there, don't care.' One such line came from the mouth of Nice Guy Eddie: 'Don't you call me an asshole.'

His Death

Chris Penn was found dead in bed by his housekeeper in his Santa Monica apartment on 24 January 2006. He was 40 years old. The autopsy showed that the primary cause of death was 'nonspecific cardiomyopathy' (heart disease). The toxicology report revealed that he had morphine, marijuana, codeine, promethazine and Valium in his system.

Penn's death occurred the day before *The Darwin Awards* – in which he plays Tom, an ice-fishing numskull who accidentally shoots his friend – premiered at the Sundance Film Festival. *Holly* was released the same year and *King of Sorrow* a year later, in 2007. It wasn't until 2013 – seven years after his death – that his final movie, *Aftermath*, came out. It features a dedication to the actor during the end credits. The film had a lukewarm reception from critics, with some calling Penn 'unconvincing' and 'overweight'.

This wasn't the only media outlet that was uncomplimentary towards the late actor. When the news of his death was reported, some articles dismissed him as 'only' Sean Penn's brother, his own career and achievements completely brushed aside. Some highlighted his run-ins with the law, wild antics and less-than-successful movie choices. An article entitled 'Let Us Praise Chris Penn' – posted on news site SFGate – found this to be 'an unfair end to a unique career', stating: 'It was as if he were the Billy Carter of Hollywood – spending his life getting busted on Sunset Boulevard and bumming cash off his Oscar-winning brother.'

Chris's funeral was held at Holy Cross Cemetery in Culver City, California, with many of Hollywood's elite in attendance, including Jack Nicholson, Tim

Robbins, James Gandolfini, Charlie Sheen, Robin Wright, Tom Sizemore, Robert Downey Jr. and Mark Ruffalo. His good buddy and 'liquor-store partner in crime' Michael Madsen was a pallbearer. The star later said he 'cried for days and days' after Chris died, continuing: 'They don't make people like that any more.' Sean Penn was similarly devastated about Chris's death and likened losing his brother to 'losing an arm'. Madsen dedicated his photography and poetry book *Signs of Life* to his sorely missed friend. Sadly, Madsen himself died on 3 July 2025, at the age of 67, from a cardiac arrest. Penn's funeral was disrupted by a paparazzo trying to get some shots. Mark Ruffalo and Sean were reportedly involved in a 'scuffle' with the photographer, during which Ruffalo took the memory card from the camera.

Chris is buried next to his father Leo at the Holy Cross Cemetery, the same resting place as many other stars, including Rita Hayworth, Sharon Tate, John Candy and Bing Crosby. When Penn's mother Eileen died in 2022, at the age of 94, she was also buried there.

Matthew Perry

Age of death: 54

Date of death: 28 October 2023

Cause of death: Acute effects of ketamine

'Well, what do you know, I guess I'll be the one who dies first'
– Matthew Perry as Chandler Bing

His Life

Matthew Perry didn't just *play* Chandler Bing. Matthew Perry *was* Chandler Bing. Smart, self-deprecating and hilariously funny, both the actor and his character as one part of the six-strong cast of hit TV show *Friends* used humour to disguise the pain that sat behind their facade. But, unlike Chandler, who got his happily ever after with Monica, Perry never found true happiness. Instead, he found drugs and an out-of-control addiction that blighted his existence. In fact, when filming Chandler and Monica's wedding in 2001 – which was perhaps the highest and most iconic point in his career – Perry was in rehab and had to be driven back to his treatment centre once he'd finished shooting his scenes.

When you consider the depths of Perry's addiction – fifty-five Vicodin pills a day; stealing from medicine cabinets during open houses; alcohol-induced pancreatitis; a burst colon from opioid abuse, resulting in a colostomy bag for nine months; fourteen stomach surgeries; an estimated $9 million spent trying to get sober – it's a wonder his career didn't implode. But, other than his fluctuating weight, he hid his struggles well, resulting in phenomenal success.

He was nominated for a Golden Globe (for his role in *The Ron Clark Story*, also known as *The Triumph*), plus five Primetime Emmy Awards (including for Outstanding Guest Actor in a Drama Series for his role in *The West Wing*). In 2000, he was in the number-one TV show (*Friends*) and the number-one film (*The Whole Nine Yards*) and, in 2002, Perry and his five *Friends* castmates – Jennifer Aniston, David Schwimmer, Courteney Cox, Matt LeBlanc and Lisa Kudrow – made history when they began commanding $1 million each per episode. On the small screen, Perry made guest appearances in other hit TV shows, including *Ally McBeal*, *Scrubs*, *The Simpsons, The Good Wife* and *The Good Fight*, and – after *Friends* finished its ten-year run in 2004 – he starred in *Studio 60 on the Sunset Strip, Go On, Mr Sunshine* and *The Odd Couple* (the latter two shows he also wrote). While TV seemed to be where he was most comfortable, Perry also lit up the big screen with his trademark wit, in movies such as *Fools Rush In, Three to Tango, Birds of America, 17 Again*, the aforementioned *The Whole Nine Yards* and its sequel *The Whole Ten Yards*. He shared the screen with his actor father – John Bennett Perry – on a fair few occasions, too. The pair played father and son twice: in the episode of *Scrubs* titled 'My Unicorn', which Matthew also directed; and in the romcom *Fools Rush In*. They also appeared in the 1993 *Home Free* and *Mr Sunshine* together. John, who became recognizable in the 1970s as the sailor in the Old Spice commercials, also popped up in the *Friends* episode 'The One With Rachel's New Dress', playing Joshua's (Tate Donovan's) dad.

It was on the set of *The Whole Nine Yards* that a friendship with Bruce Willis blossomed. Matty (as his friends called him) and Bruce would party hard, then talk about life, love and family as the sun rose, after everyone else had left. It was this friendship that led to Willis making a guest appearance in *Friends*. Willis hadn't been sure that the movie would be a success, so Perry had encouraged him to bet on it. If he lost, he'd act in *Friends*. Sure enough, *The Whole Nine Yards* went on to be a box-office smash, making $106 million worldwide, and Bruce Willis went on to scoop a Primetime Emmy for Outstanding Guest Actor in a Comedy Series for his performance as Paul Stevens in *Friends*. A win-win if ever there was one. Many years before this, another of Perry's famous friends was River Phoenix, who he had starred with in the 1988 *A Night in the Life of Jimmy Reardon*. It was Perry's film debut and the two young actors became firm friends on set. Perry described Phoenix as beautiful, and acknowledged with sadness that it seems the most talented people go down first.

Around 2016, Matthew wrote the theatre production *The End of Longing* (which he also starred in), which played both in London's West End and New York's Broadway. This wasn't Perry's first time on the stage, however. In 2003, he'd starred alongside Minnie Driver in the West End's *Sexual Perversity in Chicago*. And, ten years prior to this, after filming the *Friends* pilot and waiting for it to air, he'd spent the summer of 1993 performing at the Williamstown Theater Festival in Massachusetts alongside a then-unknown Gwyneth Paltrow. In his international best-selling memoir *Friends, Lovers, and the Big Terrible Thing*, Perry revealed that he'd made out with Gwyneth Paltrow in a closet. In an Instagram post after his death, Paltrow described their dalliance a little more romantically: 'We drove out to swim in creeks, had beers in the local college bar, kissed in a field of long grass'. She described their summer spent together as 'magical' and said that Perry was 'so funny and so sweet and so much fun to be with'.

Perry kissed a lot of other women, too. He dated actresses Yasmine Bleeth, Neve Campbell, Lauren Graham, Lizzy Caplan and Natasha Wagner (Natalie Wood's daughter), as well as professional volleyball player Rachel Dunn. He was engaged to literary manager Molly Hurwitz but called their relationship quits before they made it down the aisle. He was romantically self-destructive, breaking up with women he loved before they had the chance to dump him. He began dating Julia Roberts shortly after she made her guest appearance in the *Friends* episode 'The One After the Superbowl', and she called him 'awfully clever and funny and handsome' in an interview on *Late Show with David Letterman*. They dated for six months, during which time Perry was certain she'd break up with him. He felt like he wasn't enough; broken and not worthy of love.

Having been an alcoholic since the age of 14, Perry had felt broken and not worthy of love most of his life. Deciding against a career as a professional tennis player (he was nationally ranked in Canada – where he grew up – at the age of 13), he had thought that fame would fill the void he felt inside. But, even when 52.5 million people were watching him in the *Friends* finale, he still felt hopeless. When talking about his drug addiction, he'd recognized that it was probably going to kill him. In and out of rehab fifteen times over the years, in detox sixty-five times, and having attended approximately 6,000 Alcoholic Anonymous meetings, Perry became an advocate for rehabilitation and a spokesperson for the National Association of Drug Court Professionals. In 2013, he received the Champion of Recovery Award from the White House Office of National Drug Control Policy for opening Perry House, a men's sober-living facility in his former mansion in Malibu. During his appearance on *Q with Tom Power* in November 2022, he talked about how he wanted to be remembered when he died. He didn't want *Friends* to be the first thing people talked about; he wanted the fact that he helped others to be. And he declared that he'd spend the rest of his time on the planet proving that.

His Death

On 28 October 2023, Matthew Perry, aged 54, was found unresponsive in his hot tub at his Los Angeles home. An autopsy revealed the cause of death was due to 'acute effects of ketamine'. Other factors that contributed to his death included coronary artery disease, the effects of the opioid buprenorphine, and drowning. Perry's funeral was held at Forest Lawn Memorial Park, the resting place for a number of other celebrities, including Carrie Fisher, Paul Walker, Walt Disney and Stan Laurel. The private ceremony lasted two hours and was attended by around twenty people – including his five *Friends* co-stars and his five half-siblings (his parents divorced when he was 1 year old and went on to have other families). Peter Gabriel and Kate Bush's song 'Don't Give Up' played, which Perry had previously said would be the soundtrack to his memoir.

The day after his death, flowers, candles and other tributes – such as a single cigarette – were left outside his home in LA and the apartment block in New York known as the '*Friends* building' as it was used for an exterior shot in the show. Handwritten notes read: 'The one where we lost a friend', 'Thank you for being our friend' and 'Rest in peace Miss Chanandler Bong' (a reference to one of Chandler's hilarious scenes). During the 2023 Emmys' In Memoriam segment, Perry received a goosebump-inducing tribute as The War and Treaty duo, and singer Charlie Puth, performed an emotional version of the *Friends* theme tune 'I'll Be There For You'. Perry's image was the last to appear on the screen on stage – following many others in the entertainment industry who had died that year, including Kirstie Alley, Barbara Walters, Bob Barker, Angela Lansbury and Suzanne Somers – and was given the biggest cheer from the audience. He was also honoured in the In Memoriam section of the 2024 Academy Awards, while Italian tenor Andrea Bocelli and his son Matteo gave a moving performance of 'Time to Say Goodbye'.

The Matthew Perry Foundation was set up in the actor's honour to help those struggling with addiction. *Friends* co-creator Marta Kauffman said that Perry had wanted to 'help other addicts and it gave him purpose'. David Crane – the other *Friends* co-creator – agreed: '[Helping other addicts] absolutely became his purpose, his reason for being.'

Perry didn't just change the lives of the individuals he helped to get sober; he also changed the way America – and other English-speaking countries – communicated. He talked in such a way, hitting unusual emphases, that had never been heard in sitcoms before. At the time, he didn't realize the impact he was having, but his 'Could I BE…?' expression was to become commonplace in society for the next few decades.

Sure enough, both Jennifer Aniston and David Schwimmer included this turn of phrase in their Instagram posts remembering their good friend and co-star. Aniston said: 'Matty, I love you so much and I know you are now completely at peace and out of any pain. I talk to you every day… sometimes I can almost hear you saying "could you BE any crazier?"' Meanwhile, Schwimmer concluded his heartfelt post with: 'I imagine you up there, somewhere… looking around – "Could there BE any more clouds?"'

River Phoenix

Age of death: 23
Date of death: 31 October 1993
Cause of death: Drug overdose

'I'd rather quit while I was ahead. There's no need in overstaying your welcome.'

His Life

River Phoenix was ahead of his time. Vegan A-listers who care deeply about the environment and use their celebrity status as a platform are a dime a dozen these days, but when the young, idealistic Phoenix stormed the Hollywood scene in the 1980s and early 1990s, with his PETA (People for the Ethical Treatment of Animals) fundraising, anger towards people who drank Diet Coke and assertion that he 'wouldn't eat a hamburger for $40,000', he was an anomaly. He was known for being sensitive, eco-friendly and clean-living. Heck, he cared so deeply, he even ran out of a fancy Manhattan restaurant in tears because his then-girlfriend Martha Plimpton (who he starred with in *The Mosquito Coast* and *Running on Empty*) ordered soft-shell crab. Which is why his death – a drug overdose in a dingy LA nightclub – came as such a shock to the world. One newspaper pointed out the tragic irony by describing it as a 'clean life, dirty death'.

Born in a log cabin on a mint farm in Madras, Oregon, River was named after the 'river of life' in Herman Hesse's novel *Siddhartha*. His siblings had similarly 'at one with nature' names – Rain, Leaf (now Joaquin), Liberty and Summer. The Phoenix family lived a transient life, moving more than forty times by the time River was 18, and none of the children attended school. Their surname was originally Bottom but their parents decided to change it to Phoenix in 1977 to signify a 'rising of the ashes' – or, perhaps, a simple rebranding when they relocated to Florida, having previously been part of the cult Children of God (now known as The Family International) in South America, where their father was the sect's 'Archbishop of Venezuela'. Rain and River would play music and sing on the streets for money; their natural flair saw them winning local talent shows and, when they moved to Los Angeles in 1978, it wasn't long before fame came knocking.

At the age of 10, River was acting in commercials, for brands such as Ocean Spray, Mitsubishi and Saks Fifth Avenue, but was soon hired to play one of the younger brothers in the TV series *Seven Brides for Seven Brothers*. Phoenix's film career took off in 1985 with the release of family adventure *Explorers*, co-starring a fresh-faced Ethan Hawke. But it was the following year's *Stand By Me* – in which the blond-haired, blue-eyed actor played a good-hearted kid from the wrong side of the tracks – that made the 14-year-old River Phoenix a household name. 'When River came in to audition,' said the film's director Rob Reiner, 'it was obvious that he was just an amazing, amazing talent.' (Reiner himself met a tragic end on 14 December 2025, when he and his wife were murdered in their Los Angeles home.) The roles that followed for Phoenix – including a young Indiana Jones in *Indiana Jones and the Last Crusade*, a homeless gay hustler in *My Own Private Idaho*, and a hacking genius in *Sneakers* – solidified him as a bona fide movie star. He received an Oscar nomination for Best Actor in a Supporting Role for the 1988 *Running on Empty*, making him, at age 18, the sixth-youngest nominee in the category (with Justin Henry, at 8, being the youngest for *Kramer vs. Kramer*). Phoenix won many other accolades in his short career, including Young Artist Awards for *Stand By Me* and *The Mosquito Coast*. Peter Weir, who directed Phoenix in *The Mosquito Coast* said, 'He was obviously going to be a movie star… It's something apart from the acting ability. Laurence Olivier never had what River had.'

As well as his incredible acting ability, Phoenix was also a skilled musician (and, randomly, tap dancer), who had begun teaching himself guitar at the age of 5. Although he may have started his music career on a street corner performing for change, he progressed to playing Beethoven on the piano in *Running on Empty*, then formed a band called Aleka's Attic in which he played guitar, wrote songs and sang. One of the band's songs, 'Too Many Colors', featured in *My Own Private Idaho*. Songs that Phoenix had written and performed by himself made it onto the big screen in films he starred in, too, like 'Heart to Get' in *A Night in the Life of Jimmy Reardon* (which was slashed from the original film but reinstated years later in the director's cut) and 'Lone Star State of Mine' in *The Thing Called Love* (his last completed movie before his death).

Phoenix was naturally shy and didn't enjoy the publicity side of fame. He wasn't comfortable with the Los Angeles 'scene', saying of the city: 'You start disintegrating, and you can't see yourself, and you just feel like you're being absorbed into a big blob of glitter.' He grew weary of journalists' questions and, in an interview just ten days before he died, admitted to purposefully toying with the media by contradicting himself and fabricating things. He said that people may read various articles about him and think, 'This guy is schizophrenic'. One of the more disturbing things he told a reporter was that he was raped at the age of 4, while a member of the Children of God. Years later, his brother Joaquin said this was entirely untrue: 'It was a complete and total joke. It was just fucking with the press… because he was so tired of being asked ridiculous questions.'

The feeling across the movie industry was that the best was yet to come from River Phoenix. After directing him in *Running on Empty*, director Sidney Lumet was so impressed by his talent that he said the world was his oyster.

His Death

In the early hours of 31 October 1993 – Halloween night – the scene outside The Viper Room nightclub (then partly owned by Johnny Depp) on Los Angeles' Sunset Boulevard was one of panic, fear and Hollywood cliché. Having taken a fatal combination of cocaine and heroin – known as a 'speedball' – Phoenix had stumbled outside the club, collapsed and begun having seizure after seizure. He apparently slurred to the doorman on his way out, 'I'm gonna die, dude'. River's brother Joaquin called 911 while their sister Rain tried to administer mouth-to-mouth and sprawled on River's body in a vain attempt to stop him from convulsing. River's girlfriend Samantha Mathis (who he co-starred in *The Thing Called Love* with) was also there. As was Flea from The Red Hot Chilli Peppers, who had been performing on stage with the rest of the band that night. Paramedics arrived and took the young actor to Cedars-Sinai Medical Center, by which time he was in full cardiac arrest with no blood pressure or pulse. The 23-year-old star was pronounced dead at 1.51 am.

The next day, fans converted the outside of the nightclub into a makeshift shrine, leaving pictures, flowers, candles, poems and messages scrawled on the pavement and walls, such as 'The Eternal River' and 'River was real and always stood for truth'. The club remained closed for a week, and Depp would close it every year on 31 October as a sign of respect to the late actor.

Phoenix's untimely, abrupt death prompted much media coverage. He was called the 'vegan James Dean', and parallels were drawn between both talented actors who died suddenly in their early twenties. Debates ensued as to whether Phoenix had been a drug addict or simply an unfortunate victim of a night of partying gone horribly wrong. His mother, Aryln (which she later changed to Heart), wrote an open letter that was published in the *Los Angeles Times*. It said: 'River was not a regular drug user… the excitement and energy of the

Halloween nightclub and party scene were way beyond his usual experience and control. How many other beautiful young souls… have died using drugs recreationally?' Yet rumours circulated that Phoenix had gotten into drugs around the time he was filming *My Own Private Idaho*. Sources claimed the star had a major drug problem and *Stand By Me* co-star Corey Feldman concluded, 'Anybody that does enough drugs to OD is somebody that's a drug addict.' Feldman was no stranger to drugs himself, and when he'd previously been busted for the possession of heroin, Phoenix had commented that taking drugs is a widespread disease; not just something done by bad guys and lowlifes.

Phoenix's body was cremated at Milam Funeral Home in Gainesville, Florida, where he had lived with his family on a ranch. At the time of his death, he had recorded fifteen songs on a demo tape and was close to signing a record contract. These songs were played at the memorial service held in Gainesville, where Dan Aykroyd (who Phoenix had co-starred with in *Sneakers*), R.E.M.'s Michael Stipe and Red Hot Chilli Pepper's Flea had attended. In his coffin, the actor-cum-musician-cum-environmentalist was dressed in an Aleka's Attic T-shirt. His ashes are said to be scattered both on the Florida ranch and in a river in Montezuma, Costa Rica, where he owned property and had bought 800 acres of endangered rainforest.

Phoenix had been due to start filming *Interview with a Vampire*, but died two weeks before shooting began. He had been cast as Daniel Molloy, the interviewer, but was replaced with Christian Slater. Slater was paid $250,000 for the role and donated the entire amount to two of Phoenix's favourite charities, Earth Save and Earth Trust. There is a dedication to Phoenix after the end credits of the film. Phoenix had been in the middle of filming *Dark Blood* when he'd died and the thriller was shelved for nineteen years, until it was released – incomplete – in 2012. A few key scenes were missing but director George Sluizer 'filled in the gaps' with narration.

Samantha Mathis remained publicly silent about the death of her boyfriend until 2018, twenty-five years after that awful night. In the interview she gave to *The Guardian*, she remembered him as 'sensitive and obsessive' and said that 'he felt things on his heart very deeply'. She pondered what he might be doing if he were still alive. 'I think he'd be acting, directing, saving the environment, just living and hanging out,' she'd said. 'Oh gosh, wouldn't that be nice?'

Elvis Presley

Age of death: 42

Date of death: 16 August 1977

Cause of death: Heart failure

'Every time I think that I'm getting old, and gradually going to the grave, something else happens.'

His Life

For some, reading Elvis Presley's name in this book would be a travesty. *'He's not dead!'* they'd exclaim. *'I saw him last week!'* Indeed, the conspiracy theory that Elvis didn't die, but instead went into hiding, has meant that countless 'sightings' of the icon have been recorded over the years: at California's Legoland, as an extra in *Home Alone*, even attending his own eighty-second birthday celebrations as a white-bearded man surrounded by bodyguards at his former home, Graceland. While some find comfort in their belief that Elvis lives on, the vast majority of the world's population are of the opinion that he has, in fact, passed through the pearly gates – joining his identical twin brother, Jesse Garon Presley, who arrived thirty-five minutes before him, stillborn.

Prior to becoming known as 'The King of Rock and Roll', the quiff-haired, lip-curled, rubber-legged, hip-swivelling heartthrob had many other nicknames: The King of Western Bop... The Memphis Flash... The Hillbilly Cat... Elvis the Pelvis... It was his gyrating pelvis that had concerned adults and religious leaders in the 1950s shaking their heads, while adoring teenagers lost theirs.

But it wasn't just his provocative moves that got people's attention. It was also his sound. An intoxicating – yet, at the time, confusing – blend of rhythm and blues and country, many radio stations initially refused to play Elvis's music. Country-music DJs thought he sounded too much like a Black artist, while R&B stations thought he sounded too much like a hillbilly. The mix ultimately became known as 'rockabilly', with his hit 'Heartbreak Hotel' reaching number one in the US charts in 1956. Within a year, RCA Records had sold ten million Elvis Presley singles. Music icon Bob Dylan once said: 'Hearing [Elvis] for the first time was like busting out of jail.'

Television appearances soon followed, and it wasn't long before Hollywood came knocking. Elvis starred in more than thirty films, including *Love Me Tender*, *Jailhouse Rock*, *Viva Las Vegas*, *Tickle Me*, *Blue Hawaii* and *Girls! Girls! Girls!*. Speaking of girls, Presley was never short of admirers and was romantically linked to actresses Natalie Wood, Cybill Shepherd, Connie Stevens, Rita Moreno and Peggy Lipton, who said Elvis 'kissed like a god'. He met Priscilla Beaulieu in Germany (where he was stationed whilst serving in the United States Army) when she was 14 and he 24. Eight years later, on 1 May 1967, they married. They divorced in 1973, having had one daughter, Lisa Marie Presley. Lisa Marie sadly died on 12 January 2023, aged 54, following a cardiac arrest.

After leaving the Army in 1960, Elvis returned to acting with *G.I. Blues*, just one of his many movies in which he sings, smoulders and gets the girl. His filming schedule was gruelling, often starring in three movies a year. Elvis's musical comedies were described as 'assembly-line' and 'formulaic' – many accompanied by soundtrack albums sung by the star – and were almost all universally panned. Elvis wanted more meaty roles – and was offered lead parts in *West Side Story*, *Midnight Cowboy* and *A Star is Born* – but his manager Colonel Tom Parker turned them down. However, the movies that Elvis *did* star in always made money. Hal Wallis, who produced nine of Elvis's movies, stated: 'A Presley picture is the only sure thing in Hollywood.'

The other sure thing in Presley's life was his entourage – the 'Memphis Mafia' – who surrounded the singer throughout his career. Some were paid employees; others friends/hangers-on. They adopted the acronym 'TCB', meaning 'Taking Care of Business', and Elvis and Priscilla even created a logo with this abbreviation and a lightning bolt, inspired by a flight taken during stormy conditions. This logo adorned the tail of Elvis's private jet, plus gold and diamond necklaces and rings that he would give as gifts. Such pieces now sell for hundreds of thousands at auction.

Despite being one of the most famous people in the world, Elvis only ever performed in one other country besides America – Canada. Much to the chagrin of fans across the globe, Parker put the kibosh on any notion of touring internationally… and the reason why only emerged after Elvis's death. It was discovered that his manager had immigrated to the States illegally from the Netherlands (disappearing the same night that a murder took place on his family's street). He changed his name from Andreas Cornelis van Kuijk and never held a US passport. Parker took fifty per cent of his client's earnings, when at the time the industry standard was ten per cent.

In his heyday, Elvis was unstoppable. His 'Love Me Tender' ballad inspired a record-breaking million advance orders; he commanded $1 million a year to perform in Vegas; he was awarded the Recording Academy Lifetime Achievement Award (then called the Bing Crosby Award) in 1971; and won a Grammy Lifetime Achievement Award at age 36. But by the time his divorce from Priscilla was finalized, his fall from Grace(land) was in full swing. The once-dazzling star had become overweight and addicted to all manner of drugs, including barbiturates, pethidine, antihistamines, tranquilizers, sedatives and sleeping pills – overdosing a couple of times and even spending time in a coma. He became afflicted with high blood pressure, liver damage, glaucoma, extreme constipation and an enlarged colon. On stage, he cut his concerts short and was often incoherent. Some might say that before he'd even died, Elvis had already 'left the building'.

His Death

Elvis Presley's death was (and still is, if you're in the 'Elvis lives' camp) shrouded in mystery. But it was declared after his death on 16 August 1977 that he had simply died from heart failure, aged 42, after his fiancée Ginger Alden found him face-down on his bathroom floor, having fallen from the toilet. The doctor who issued Elvis's death certificate stated that 'prescription drugs found in his blood were not a contributing factor', but it came to light that this was not actually the case. Fourteen drugs had been found in Elvis's system, ten in significant quantities. It later emerged that Elvis had been prescribed almost 9,000 pills, vials and injections in the seven months before his death. It seemed that drugs had indeed played an integral part in Elvis's demise and the original 'cause of death' had come at the request of his mortified family, who didn't want his reputation sullied.

His family had a private autopsy carried out, the results of which were to remain sealed for fifty years. All will be revealed in 2027 but, until then, there are a couple of other theories as to how Elvis ultimately died. One: constipation. He had been 'blocked up' for some four months as a result of his drug use and high-fat diet, and while trying in vain for a bowel movement, his abdominal aorta was compressed, shutting down his heart. Two: a head injury. In 1967, ten years prior to his death, Elvis tripped over a television cord and knocked himself unconscious on a bathtub. This is said to have triggered a progressive autoimmune inflammatory disorder meaning that, over the years, Elvis developed issues such as vertigo, insomnia, headaches, eye infections, jaundice, plus pain in his lungs, liver, heart, spine and bowels. Retired homicide detective and forensic coroner Garry Rodgers told *HuffPost* that he would have chalked up Elvis's death to 'cardiac arrhythmia antecedent to hypertensive cardiovascular disease with atherosclerotic heart disease antecedent to polypharmacy antecedent to autoimmune inflammatory disorder antecedent to traumatic brain injury', which, in layman's terms translates to: 'a heart attack caused by heart disease and drug use caused by an autoimmune disease, which was sparked by a brain injury'.

On 18 August, two days after his death, Elvis's funeral was held at Graceland. The procession attracted some 80,000 fans, with 30,000 people filing past his open casket to pay their respects. Whilst fans were mourning, more tragedy ensued that day, when a car ploughed into the crowd, killing two women and critically injuring a third. Elvis was buried next to his mother, Gladys, at Forest Hill Cemetery but, after an attempt was made to steal his body two weeks later, both he and his ma were exhumed and reburied in Graceland's Meditation Garden. Branded with his 'TCB lightning-bolt' logo, Elvis's gravestone, in part, reads: 'He revolutionized the field of music… He became a living legend in his own time… God saw that he needed some rest and called him home to be with Him'.

While Elvis has been resting, his music and memory have lived on. The Guinness World Records cite him as the best-selling solo artist of all time, reaching sales of around one billion worldwide. Since 2001, according to *Forbes*, he has been amongst the top seven highest-paid dead celebrities, hitting number one many times, including in 2002, when a remix of 'A Little Less Conversation' was used in a Nike advertising campaign during the FIFA World Cup. His estate earned as much as US $60 million during 2010, the year *Viva Elvis: The Album* was released. Indeed, even though Elvis has been gone for many decades, he's still setting the charts – and hearts – ablaze. He has been inducted into an array of music halls of fame, including the Rock & Roll Hall of Fame, Country Music Hall of Fame, Gospel Hall of Fame and Rockabilly Hall of Fame. Graceland was opened to the public in 1982 and has become the second-most-visited home in the US, after the White House, attracting more than half a million visitors every year. It was designated a National Historic Landmark in 2006, and hosts the annual Elvis Week, held every August around the anniversary of his death. The celebration attracts fans from all over the world, who enjoy concerts, Elvis-impersonator competitions, tours of the mansion, dance parties and a candlelit vigil at Elvis's gravesite.

Elvis is also still lighting up the screen – big and small. Netflix's 2023 animated series *Agent Elvis* (co-produced by Priscilla Presley) sees Elvis – voiced by Matthew McConaughey – swapping his jumpsuit for a jetpack to fight crime; and Baz Luhrmann's 2022 *Elvis* was the second-highest-grossing musical biopic in terms of global box-office sales, after *Bohemian Rhapsody*. Tom Hanks played Colonel Tom Parker, and said of the legend: 'Look, Elvis was Picasso. He was a one-of-a-kind, once-in-a-lifetime artist.' Luhrmann followed up his biopic with *EPiC: Elvis Presley in Concert*, which had its first advance screening at Graceland on 8 January 2026, which would have been the performer's ninety-first birthday. The concert documentary showcases Elvis's unrivalled stage presence, magnetism and raw talent from the iconic 1970s Vegas years, and is narrated by Elvis himself via archive footage.

Any way you slice it, The King lives on.

Kelly Preston

Age of death: 57

Date of death: 12 July 2020

Cause of death: Breast cancer

'I would like to end world hunger and create world peace.'

Her Life

You may not have sat up and taken notice of Kelly Preston until her performance as Avery in the 1996 *Jerry Maguire*, in which she sucker-punched Tom Cruise and called him a loser after being dumped by him. But having started her acting career in 1980 with a part in television series *Hawaii Five-0*, Preston was a Hollywood fixture for decades – appearing in films such as *Twins* alongside Arnold Schwarzenegger, *Addicted to Love* next to Meg Ryan, and *For Love of the Game* with Kevin Costner.

She was considered by many to be an underrated actress, never reaching her true potential on screen. Having played roles in more than sixty television shows and movies, this may have been a conscious decision – she once said, 'Keeping it all normal and keeping us together is my first priority. Then I fit films into my life.' The 'us' who she referred to was her family: husband John Travolta and their children. Tragically, their oldest son Jett died after a seizure in 2009 at the age of 16 while on holiday in The Bahamas, leaving the family, including their daughter Ella Bleu, devastated. Two years later, John and Kelly had another son, Benjamin.

Born in Honolulu, Hawaii, Preston's birth name was Kelly Kamalelehua Smith. Kamalelehua means 'garden of lehuas' (a lehua is a bright red bloom that plays a major role in Hawaiian culture). She attended Punahou School at the same time as Barack Obama, who graduated there in 1979, a year before Preston. Other famous alumni include actress Joan Blondell, who appeared in more than 100 film and TV productions, and has a star on the Hollywood Walk of Fame; and actor Buster Crabbe, who played Tarzan, Flash Gordon and Buck Rogers in the 1930s.

Preston met Travolta on the set of the 1989 comedy film *The Experts*, while she was married to *SpaceCamp* co-star Kevin Gage. The scene in which their characters meet sees Travolta asking, 'Does anybody here know how to dance?', to which a seductive Preston replies, 'I know how to dance'. Turns out, after her divorce, she and John would dance together for almost twenty-nine years. Dancing was a big part of their marriage (people don't call him 'snake hips Travolta' for nothing, with his top moves coming out in *Grease*, *Saturday Night Fever*, even *Pulp Fiction*). '[We dance] all the time… I love it,' said Preston.

The couple appeared in four other movies together – *Battlefield Earth*, *Old Dogs*, *From Paris With Love* and *Gotti*. Their daughter Ella Bleu was also in *Old Dogs*. None did well at the box office, or with critics, and Preston even earned herself a Golden Raspberry Award (Razzie) as Worst Supporting Actress for her performance in *Battlefield Earth*. The sci-fi action film was based on the novel of the same name, written by L. Ron Hubbard, the founder of the Church of Scientology. Both active Scientologists, Preston and Travolta were married by a French Scientologist minister when they eloped to Paris in 1991 (a week later they had a second wedding ceremony in Florida to make it legal).

Prior to her relationship with Travolta, Preston had lived with George Clooney and had been engaged to Charlie Sheen. As a present for her birthday, Clooney gave Preston a pot-bellied pig called Max, who he retained custody of when the couple split. Her relationship with Sheen (who had proposed with a twenty-five-carat, $200,000 diamond engagement ring) came to an end shortly after he allegedly shot her in the wrist. It was only twenty-one years later that she spoke publicly about the incident, explaining that it had been a complete accident – Charlie hadn't shot her but the gun had gone off after being dropped on the floor.

Ella Bleu is following in her parents' footsteps by taking to the big screen, having starred alongside her dad and Morgan Freeman in the 2019 *The Poison Rose* (released internationally as *Eye for an Eye*). Proud mum took to Instagram to congratulate her daughter: 'Still in absolute awe of my stunning daughter… She has jumped into the "family business" as an absolute natural'. Preston's last ever Instagram post also celebrated her family she adored so much. To mark Father's Day, she posted a family selfie and a photo of Travolta with Jett, saying: 'Happy Father's Day to the best one I know, we love you.'

Her Death

Preston battled breast cancer privately for two years, before dying at her Florida home on 12 July 2020, at the age of 57. She had not widely publicized her illness, and was supported by close family and friends. Travolta announced his wife's death with a heartfelt message on Instagram by saying, 'She fought a courageous fight… Kelly's love and life will always be remembered… I will be taking some time to be there for my children who have lost their mother, so forgive me in advance if you don't hear from us for a while. All my love, JT.'

This wasn't the first time Travolta had been left grief-stricken by cancer. In 1977, his first love, Diana Hyland, who he starred with in *The Boy in the Plastic Bubble*, died in his arms from breast cancer. Good friend and *Grease* co-star Olivia Newton-John also battled breast cancer from 1992 until her death in August 2022, having previously set up the Olivia Newton-John Foundation to help others suffering with the disease. After Preston's death, she tweeted a photo of the two of them and said, 'Kelly was a radiant, warm and gentle spirit – a loving, devoted wife, mother and sweet friend… Kelly's light shines on in her beautiful children.'

Friends, former co-stars and the Hollywood elite paid tribute to Preston, with Russell Crowe describing her as a 'sparkly eyed gem', and Kirstie Alley tweeting, 'Kelly… you are Hawaii and I am Kansas. The perfect combination for best friends. I love you forever Shooster… so here's to "until we meet again somewhere",' along with the song 'Somewhere Over the Rainbow'. (Two years later, on 5 December 2022, Kirstie Alley died from colon cancer.) Sharon Stone said, 'The loss of Kelly Preston is like losing sunshine', while Arnold Schwarzenegger called her 'extraordinary', with a talent that was 'off the charts'.

A few weeks after Preston's death, her doting husband posted a touching video on social media of him and Ella Bleu dancing, saying, 'My daughter @ella.travolta and I dancing in memory of momma. One of Kelly's favorite things, dancing with me.' In September 2024, Ella Beau released her song 'Little Bird', which is a tribute to her much-missed mum. The music video includes touching home videos of the family at birthday parties, on holiday and dancing together. In an interview with *Access Hollywood*, Ella Bleu talked of how 'fun and exciting and wonderful' her mum made every situation, every holiday, every birthday. 'Every activity was so heightened because of the life she put into it.'

Christopher Reeve

Age of death: 52

Date of death: 10 October 2004

Cause of death: Heart failure

'You play the hand you're dealt. I think the game's worthwhile.'

His Life

Is it a bird? Is it a plane? No, it's Superman! Christopher Reeve, best known for playing the 'Man of Steel' in the 1978 *Superman* and three subsequent sequels was, undoubtedly, a super man. The strapping 6 ft 4 in New Yorker cheated death many times. Indeed, it's a wonder it's not written above: 'Age of death: 42; Cause of death: Horse-riding accident'. Or 'Cause of death: Suicide… Anaphylactic shock… Bone marrow infection…'.

On 27 May 1995, Reeve was thrown from his horse in an equestrian competition. He was left paralyzed from the neck down, destined to be in a wheelchair for the rest of his life. Five days after the accident, he regained full consciousness and, unable to breathe without the aid of a ventilator, mouthed to his wife Dana, 'Maybe we should let me go.' She tearfully responded that she would support whatever decision he made, adding, 'You're still you.' Following this conversation and visits from his children, however, Reeve consented to life-saving surgery and began the long road to accepting his fate and carving out a life no one evers imagines they'll be living. The grim reaper came knocking a few more times; once when Reeve's body reacted badly to the drug Sygen, sending it into anaphylactic shock, and a few times when infections starting in his bone marrow proved to be almost fatal. But Reeve fought back with all his strength. His life became full and active again, packed with film work, television appearances, book writing, activism, public speaking, establishing the Christopher Reeve Foundation, and parenting his children, Matthew, Alexandra and Will (he had Matthew and Alexandra with long-term partner Gae Exton, and Will with wife Dana).

Rewind sixteen years to the 1979 Academy Awards, when Western-movie-star John Wayne first met Reeve. He turned to fellow actor Cary Grant and said,

'This is our new man. He's taking over.' Incidentally, Reeve based his portrayal of Clark Kent on Cary Grant's performance in *Bringing Up Baby*. Katharine Hepburn, who Reeve made his Broadway debut with in *A Matter of Gravity* in 1976, had agreed: 'You're going to be a big star, Christopher, and support me in my old age.' Although Reeve achieved great success in Hollywood ($300 million at the box office for his four *Superman* movies is nothing to sniff at), it was this success that perhaps held him back creatively and pooh-poohed Wayne's prediction. Despite the fact that Reeve took varying roles throughout his career – including a mail pilot in *The Aviator* (in which the actor and real-life pilot performed all his own stunts), a congressman in *The Remains of the Day*, and a millionaire in *Switching Channels,* he was never able to 'escape the cape', with audiences always seeing him as the comic-book hero whose jaw could cut glass.

He was picky with the characters he selected, turning down lead roles in *Splash*, *Romancing the Stone*, *American Gigolo*, *The World According to Garp*, *Body Heat* and *Lethal Weapon*. One of the roles Reeve did take, however, eerily saw life imitating art when he played a police officer who ended up paralyzed and in a wheelchair after a gunshot wound. A week after the 1995 *Above Suspicion* hit the screen, Reeve himself was paralyzed. To prepare for the role, he'd spent time at a spinal-cord trauma unit and, during an interview to promote the film, he'd contemplated, 'You can see how easily it can happen. One moment everything is fine and then the world falls apart.'

While Reeve's own world was falling apart, it had been one of his good friends who had brought him back from the brink. At an especially bleak moment, Reeve's hospital door had flown open and a man talking in a Russian accent, wearing a surgical gown and scrub hat, had announced that he was there to perform a rectal exam. It was his old roommate from Juillard performing arts school Robin Williams, re-enacting his zany character from *Nine Months*. For the first time since the accident, Reeve laughed. With the help of his old friend, he somehow knew he was going to be alright.

And alright he was. After he'd resolved to make the best of the cards he'd been dealt, although he couldn't walk, he was, in fact, flying (without the cape this time). In 1997, Reeve made his directorial debut with *In the Gloaming* starring Whoopi Goldberg, Glenn Close and Bridget Fonda, for which he was nominated for an Emmy; then in 1999 he starred in *Rear Window*, for which he was nominated for a Golden Globe and took home the Screen Actors Guild Award. He also made several appearances in the Superman-centric TV show *Smallville*, plus was in an episode of multi-award-winning legal drama *The Practice*. Reeve wrote two autobiographies, *Still Me* and

Nothing is Impossible. Still Me was on the *New York Times* bestseller list for eleven weeks in 1999, and it won a Grammy in the Best Spoken Word Album category.

Before Reeve's accident, he used his celebrity status for good, visiting terminally ill children through the Make-A-Wish Foundation, joining the board of directors for Save the Children and lending his support to Amnesty International. In 1987, he led a protest march in Santiago, Chile to help save the lives of seventy-seven actors who dictator Pinochet had threatened to execute. For his heroism, he received accolades including a Special Citation Obie Award. After Reeve's accident, his philanthropy didn't stop. As well as serving on the board of many organizations seeking to improve the lives of people with disabilities, and lobbying for an increase of government benefits for them, he also co-founded the Reeve-Irvine Research Center, which has become one of the leading spinal-cord research institutes in the world. He also set up the Christopher Reeve Foundation, which sought to fund research into spinal-cord injury and improve the quality of life of those who are paralyzed. To date, the foundation has invested more than $145 million in research and awarded more than $46 million in quality-of-life grants.

There's no denying Reeve had a fighting spirit. Yes, life dealt him a cruel blow but he chose not to give up, and in doing so he helped many, many people. There was a sign up on his wall that he lived by – it read: 'For those who said I couldn't do it, for those who said I shouldn't do it, for those who said it's impossible, see you at the finish line'.

Tragically, Reeve reached the finish line all too soon.

His Death

At the age of 52, Christopher Reeve died on 10 October 2004 at a New York hospital after being treated for a bedsore that became infected and developed into sepsis. He was given an antibiotic for the infection but went into cardiac arrest and then fell into a coma. Although no official autopsy was carried out, both Reeve's wife Dana and his doctor believed that the adverse reaction to the antibiotic caused his death. At the time of his death, Reeve's condition had improved in that he had regained partial movement in his toes and fingers, could differentiate between hot and cold temperatures, and could feel a pin prick anywhere on his body.

A few days after he died, a private ceremony was held at the star's Pound Ridge home in the suburbs of New York, attended by around 100 friends and family members. A memorial service was held at the world-renowned Juilliard

School, where Reeve had graduated in 1975. The service was attended by some 900 people, including Michael J. Fox, Susan Sarandon, Kim Cattrall, Mary Tyler Moore, Laura Linney, Larry King and Hillary Clinton, who was a senator at the time. 'His courage and inspiration will live on,' said Clinton in her speech honouring him. Broadway star Brian Stokes Mitchell sang 'The Impossible Dream' from the musical *Man of La Mancha.* The memorial ended with the Broadway cast of *The Lion King* singing 'The Circle of Life'. Those who spoke included loyal friend Robin Williams, Glenn Close and Meryl Streep. Reeve's body was cremated at Ferncliff Cemetery in New York, and another memorial service was held at the Unitarian Church in Westport, Connecticut. During the service, he was described as 'one of the brightest, informed, alert, sensitive and caring men [sic]… who smiled quickly, easily and frequently.'

Reeve's widow took over the Christopher Reeve Foundation after his death but, sadly, she was diagnosed with lung cancer in 2005 and died on 6 March 2006, aged 44. The foundation was renamed the Christopher & Dana Reeve Foundation and their children serve on the board of directors. The foundation continues to help those suffering from paralysis and maintains its mission of 'Today's Care. Tomorrow's Cure'. Will Reeve is a correspondent for *ABC News* and *Good Morning America*, and dabbled in acting before this, featuring in *The Brooke Ellison Story, In The Gloaming* and *Everyone's Hero*, all directed by his dad. He also plays a TV reporter in the 2025 *Superman.*

In January 2024, all three of Reeve's children attended the world premiere of *Super/Man: The Christopher Reeve Story* on the opening night of the Sundance Film Festival. The emotional documentary features home videos, clips of Reeve, and interviews from the actor's loved ones and fellow Hollywood stars, including Jeff Daniels, Susan Sarandon, Glenn Close and Whoopi Goldberg. The audience laughed, cried and gave the film a rousing standing ovation, drawing a parallel to the extended standing ovation the star himself had received at the 1996 Academy Awards when making his first public appearance since the accident that left him paralyzed. 'I wouldn't have missed this kind of welcome for the world,' he'd said. 'Thank you.'

After Reeve died, a number of Superman-themed cartoons were created to honour him. Many had Superman flying away from his wheelchair. Some showed Reeve arriving in heaven dressed as Superman; in one, he said, 'You can keep the wings', and in another he declined the wings again, saying, 'No thanks, I'd rather walk'. In another, a young boy in a wheelchair is saying, 'He was the Man of Steel. He had incredible vision. He used his powers to save people. Nothing could stop him. And I think before that he acted in some *Superman* movies'.

Patrick Swayze

Age of death: 57

Date of death: 14 September 2009

Cause of death: Pancreatic cancer

'The longer your life goes on, the more death you face.'

His Life

He was the man who took Baby out of the corner, made pottery erotic and suffered death by surfing. He was also the man who became a verb – to 'Swayze' someone is to leave or disappear, much like his character did in *Ghost*. But this slang term almost never got the chance to exist. Indeed, the spiritual role of Sam Wheat in the 1990 slow-burn blockbuster that earned more than $505 million at the international box office was almost never awarded to Patrick Swayze. Having just seen the muscular actor's performance as the hard-as-nails bouncer in *Road House* – where he rips a man's throat out with his bare hands and utters the tough-guy line 'Pain don't hurt' – *Ghost*'s director Jerry Zucker unequivocally stated that Swayze would not play the lead in this emotional movie. Thankfully for Swayze – and movie-goers the world over – Zucker had a change of heart and ultimately cast him over the likes of Bruce Willis, Kevin Bacon, Alec Baldwin, Tom Hanks, Mel Gibson and Paul Hogan, who were all considered for the part.

Having previously lit up the screen (and Baby's carnal desires) in *Dirty Dancing* in 1987, now with the success of *Ghost*, Swayze was well on his way to becoming typecast as 'Hollywood's hunk with a heart' – a label that he didn't want. After being voted *People* magazine's Sexiest Man Alive in 1991 and being nominated as Most Desirable Male in the MTV Movie + TV Awards, in a bid to show the world he was an 'actor' rather than a 'movie star', he was thrilled to be cast as the dispirited doctor who finds himself in the slums of Calcutta in the 1992 *City of Joy*. Unfortunately, the film wasn't as well-received as Swayze would have liked, with one critic describing it as 'well-intentioned but mostly bland'.

One of Swayze's films that wouldn't be described as bland, however, is *To Wong Foo, Thanks for Everything! Julie Newmar*, in which the butch actor dragged up to play Vida Boheme, alongside fellow queens Wesley Snipes and John Leguizamo. Swayze was nominated for a Golden Globe for his performance in this movie, as well as for *Ghost* and *Dirty Dancing*. Another of his non-bland roles was as cringey motivational speaker Jim Cunningham, who turns out to be a paedophile, in psychological drama *Donnie Darko*. In *Point Break*, he played a surfer-cum-bank robber and, as a self-confessed adrenaline junkie, performed his own sky-diving stunts. His body saw its fair share of injuries at the hands of his active pursuits; all of his ten fingers and his ankle were broken over the years, and his left knee was operated on five times. The actor was seriously injured in May 1997 while filming *Letters From a Killer* – he fell from a horse and hit a tree, breaking both his legs and suffering four detached tendons in his shoulder. Filming had to be put on hold for two months while he recovered.

In the late 1980s, Swayze struggled with his newfound stardom and began drinking heavily. He referred to these years as his 'Crazy Swayze' period and admitted he was a 'not-very-pretty drunk'. He sought rehab treatment, vowing not to destroy his career or become a Hollywood casualty. But, while still mourning the death of his father in 1982, he turned to the bottle again when his sister Vicky committed suicide in 1994. Ultimately, though, he decided to honour his sister by regaining control of his life.

Swayze – nicknamed Buddy by most people who knew him – was a man of many talents. On top of his acting ability, he was also a skilled cowboy, a gymnast, a martial arts expert, a singer/songwriter (his hit ballad 'She's Like the Wind' reached number three in the US charts; he originally co-wrote it for the 1984 teen drama *Grandview U.S.A*, which he starred in with Jamie Lee Curtis, but it ended up in *Dirty Dancing*) and, of course, an incredible dancer. Having grown up surrounded by dancing – his mum ran a ballet school and went on to choreograph dance sequences in the John Travolta film *Urban Cowboy* – he showed a natural flair for the art. When he was teased as a child by his peers, with his mother's permission, he beat them up. Recalling one incident, his brother Don said, 'Without putting down his books or violin, he did a little sweep with his legs and took both of them out. I grew up with a superhero in my family.' At the age of 19, Swayze moved from his hometown of Houston, Texas to New York to complete his formal dance training, and made his first professional appearance as a dancer and figure skater, playing Prince Charming in *Disney on Parade*. He went on to play Danny Zuko in *Grease* on Broadway; then, decades later, Billy Flynn in *Chicago* in 2003. In 2006, Swayze made his London West End debut in the musical *Guys and Dolls* as Nathan Detroit.

Swayze met Lisa Niemi at his mother's dance school when he was 18 and she was 14. They married in 1975 and were together until his death. She was the inspiration for 'She's Like the Wind'. The couple never had children, with Lisa suffering two miscarriages, which was a source of sadness for them both. They owned two ranches, one in California and one in New Mexico, where they bred Arabian horses, and kept dogs, cats, peacocks and rodeo cattle. 'It's like kids are the one thing that's missing at the ranch,' said Swayze. Although it's never been confirmed, a rumour emerged in 2017 that he had a secret love child, apparently conceived during a one-night stand in 1972.

Swayze remembers his own father, a Texas state rodeo champion, fondly, tearing up when asked about him in interviews conducted by Barbara Walters in both 1988 and 2009. The latter was carried out just a few months before Swayze died, where he discussed wanting to make the most of however long he had left. He declared that he refused to 'chase staying alive', instead opting to 'live'. And live he did, right up until the end. Having been diagnosed with advanced stage-four pancreatic cancer at the beginning of 2008 (and being given only a one per cent chance of surviving longer than five years), Swayze refused to give up, insisting he 'doesn't want to be the poster boy for living with cancer'. Filming the first season of the crime drama series *The Beast*, he would work fourteen- to sixteen-hour days and get chemotherapy on the weekends. His final film *Powder Blue* – in which he acted alongside his brother Don – was released the same year as *The Beast*, 2009. Swayze had been a heavy smoker for some forty years, sometimes smoking sixty cigarettes a day, and stated that this may have had something to do with the development of his cancer. However, he'd continued to smoke during his treatment, saying, 'When it looks like I may live longer than five minutes, I'll drop cigarettes like a hot potato.' Sadly, he never got the chance to kick the habit.

His Death

Patrick Swayze died twenty months after his cancer diagnosis, on 14 September 2009, aged 57. A memorial service was held on the Sony Studios lot in Culver City, California, where the hundreds of guests attending were greeted by a white horse owned by Swayze that had a pair of his boots facing backwards in the stirrups. This is an old horseman tradition symbolizing the rider looking back towards the living one last time. The service included many photos of Swayze on his horses, as well as a video tribute, speeches and a performance by professional dancers. Instead of flowers, the family asked that donations be made to the Stand Up to Cancer charity or The Patrick Swayze Pancreas Cancer

Research Fund. Swayze was cremated and his ashes scattered over his New Mexico ranch, Rancho de Dí as Alegres, which means 'Ranch of Happy Days'.

A memorial stone for Swayze, dedicated on 21 November 2009, sits on the grounds of Mountain Lake Hotel in Pembroke, Virginia, where *Dirty Dancing* was filmed. The stone was in the nearby lake during the filming of the movie and was taken from the spot next to where 'The Lift' was shot. After his death, *Dirty Dancing* co-star Jennifer Grey said, 'When I think of him, I think of being in his arms when we were kids, dancing, practicing the lift in the freezing lake, having a blast doing this tiny little movie we thought no one would ever see.' This 'tiny little movie' went on to gross more than $214 million worldwide and was the first film to sell one million copies on video. The iconic lift scene in the film's finale was voted the best movie dance moment of all time in a poll conducted by QVC.

Swayze was a keen environmentalist, helping to design and implement a 200-year forest stewardship plan. During his final interview with Barbara Walters, he explained that he was happy to be leaving a legacy such as this. Another environmental project that Swayze helped with was the relocation of the Gallinas River in San Miguel County, New Mexico, which had veered off course. The project greatly improved the habitat for fish and wildlife.

Friends, family, colleagues and co-stars including Demi Moore, Jennifer Grey, Rob Lowe and Lori Petty pay tribute to Swayze in the 2019 documentary *I Am Patrick Swayze*. In it, he's described as an 'open book' and a 'macho guy with the soul of a poet', who 'was passionate and intense about everything. Everything.' Demi Moore, who starred alongside him in *Ghost* as his girlfriend Molly, described him as having 'a beautiful balance between strength and softness'. Following his death, she tweeted, 'And in the words of Sam to Molly: "It's amazing, Molly. The love inside, you take it with you".'

Sharon Tate

Age of death: 26
Date of death: 9 August 1969
Cause of death: Murder

'My whole life has been decided by fate.'

Her Life

'Let's face it, all I know how to do is take off my clothes,' said Jennifer North – the alluring character played by the beautiful (sometimes naked) Sharon Tate – in the 1967 *Valley of the Dolls*. Tate also appeared nude or semi-nude in horror spoof *The Fearless Vampire Killers*, in *Playboy* in 1967, and in *Esquire* the same year. She had no qualms about showing a bit of flesh: 'I honestly don't understand the big fuss made over nudity and sex in films. It's silly.' But taking her clothes off certainly wasn't all that Tate knew how to do. The actress was so much more than a sex symbol. She was intelligent, with ambitions of studying psychiatry at college. She was spunky, performing her own stunts in *The Wrecking Crew* and being taught martial arts by Bruce Lee. She was candid, once telling a reporter, 'It's a terrible movie' when her beach film *Don't Make Waves* opened to poor reviews, adding, 'Sometimes I say things I shouldn't. I guess I'm too outspoken.'

'Outspoken' Sharon was also worldly, having lived in various countries growing up – including her home country America, Germany, England and Italy – due to her father being an officer in the US Army. It was in Italy where the beauty-pageant winner/model got bitten by the acting bug. In 1962, when Sharon was 19 years old, her father was assigned to Verona. *Hemingway's Adventures of a Young Man* starring Paul Newman was being filmed nearby and Tate got a part as an extra, as she also later did in *Barabbas*. On the set of *Hemingway's Adventures*, Tate met actor Richard Beymer (famous for his role as Tony in *West Side Story*), who introduced her to producer Martin Ransohoff. Ransohoff is given credit for having 'discovered' Tate, and gave her small television parts in *The Beverly Hillbillies* and *Mister Ed*. Tate was initially deemed too timid and lacking in confidence to land any major roles, unsuccessfully auditioning for parts such as Liesl in *The Sound of Music*. In 1965, however, Ransohoff finally gave Tate her first major movie role as Odile de Caray in *Eye of the Devil*. The next year, Tate continued down the road of 'scream queen' in *The Fearless Vampire Killers*, directed by Roman Polanski, who later became her husband.

The couple's one-and-a-half-year marriage was shrouded in rumours and speculation, with many saying Polanski forced his wife into having threesomes with random women he'd picked up. He apparently urged her to fulfil his sexual fantasies via orgies and homemade sex tapes he'd play to his friends at parties. He is also said to have controlled what clothes and make-up she wore. Speaking of her husband's infidelities, Tate told photographer Peter Evans: 'We have a good arrangement. Roman lies to me and I pretend to believe him.' After their wedding in London on 20 January 1968, Tate and Polanski returned to Los Angeles and soon became part of the trendy Hollywood crowd that included some of the biggest names in the film industry, including Warren Beatty, Joan Collins, Mia Farrow, Jane Fonda, Steve McQueen, Peter Sellers, Yul Brynner and Kirk Douglas. Evans described them as 'the imperfect couple... Cool, nomadic, talented and nicely shocking'. One thing that was just plain shocking was that Polanski allegedly wouldn't sleep with Tate after she fell pregnant with his child, and he urged her to get an abortion. She refused, so he left their LA home for London, where he is said to have had an affair with Michelle Phillips of The Mamas & The Papas.

Tate only starred in six films before her life was cut short. She was just beginning to be taken seriously as an actress to be reckoned with, receiving a Golden Globe nomination as Most Promising Newcomer for her performance in *Valley of the Dolls* (she was pipped by Katharine Ross for her role as Elaine Robinson in *The Graduate*) and placing fourth in the Golden Laurel Awards as the Female New Face. The last film she made was *12+1*, also known as *The 13 Chairs*, with reviewers describing her as 'frisky and cute' and 'delicious in her role as the antique dealer' – many were excited by the realization that she had a knack for comedy. During the *All Eyes on Sharon Tate* documentary, used to publicize *Eye of the Devil*, Tate stated: 'I don't fool myself – I can't see myself doing Shakespeare.' Instead, she had ambitions of finding a niche in light comedy, emulating the likes of Carole Lombard, Catherine Deneuve and Faye Dunaway. Many agreed that the rising star had the world at her feet. *Newsweek* wrote: 'Sharon Tate is one of the most smashing young things to hit Hollywood in a long time' and director Mark Robson told Polanski: 'That's a great girl you're living with. Few actresses have her kind of vulnerability. She's got a great future.'

Her Death

The murder of 26-year-old Sharon Tate has gone down as one of the most heinous, evil crimes in American history. On the night of 9 August 1969, the eight-and-a-half-months-pregnant actress was brutally stabbed sixteen times at her home on Cielo Drive in Los Angeles by members of the 'Manson Family', as she begged them to let her live long enough to give birth to her baby, offering herself as a hostage. The cult followers of deranged Charles Manson ignored her terrified pleas and continued with their senseless attack, writing the word 'Pig' on the front door with her blood after they had butchered her. Tate's ex-boyfriend, celebrity hairdresser Jay Sebring, coffee heiress Abigail Folger, Wojtek Fryowski (a childhood friend of Polanski) and 18-year-old Steven Parent – who was a friend of the estate's caretaker – were also victims. The bodies of Tate and Sebring were found in the living room, with a long rope around both their necks connecting them. The following evening, Leno LaBianca and his wife Rosemary were also slayed by the 'family'. The infamous killings came to be known as the Tate-LaBianca murders.

Charles Manson, Tex Watson, Susan Atkins, Patricia Krenwinkel and Linda Kasabian were found guilty of the murders and given the death penalty, which was later reduced to life sentences when California abolished capital punishment in 1972. In an interview conducted in 1976, from jail, Atkins spoke of the night of the murders, recalling that Tex had announced: 'I'm the devil and I'm here to do the devil's business.' During her 'Manson years', Atkins dropped acid at least 300 times and abused all manner of other drugs, which she believes contributed to her altered mindset during the killings. Doris Tate, Sharon's mother, campaigned passionately against the parole of each of the Manson killers and worked with victims of violent crime, becoming an advocate for their rights. In 1992, President George Bush recognized Doris as one of his 'thousand points of light' for this work. After her death, Patti Tate and Debra Tate – Sharon's sisters – picked up where their mother had left off. Greg King, who wrote *Sharon Tate and the Manson Murders*, stated: 'Sharon's real legacy lies not in her movies… The very fact that victims or their families in California are able to sit before those convicted of a crime and have a voice in the sentencing at trials… is largely due to the work of Doris [and Patti] Tate.'

Sharon's legacy also lives on through depictions of her on screen – both in films and TV shows. She has been portrayed many times by various actresses, including Amanda Brooks in *Aquarius*, Hilary Duff in *The Haunting of Sharon Tate* and Margot Robbie in Quentin Tarantino's *Once Upon a Time... in Hollywood*, for which Robbie was nominated for a BAFTA for Best Supporting

Actress. In an interview on *The Jess Cagle Show* for Sirius XM, Tarantino explained why he felt compelled to tell Sharon Tate's story in his movie. He described her as 'almost too good to be true' and a 'really nifty person', adding, 'I think it's horrible that she's been defined by her murder.' The writer/director is proud of the fact that *Once Upon a Time... in Hollywood* intrigued audiences enough to look the actress up, find out more about her and learn about Sharon Tate the person, rather than Sharon Tate the murder victim. One of her quirks was that she would often go barefoot in public. When she came across a restaurant with a 'no shoes, no service' rule, she'd put rubber bands around her ankles to make it look like she was wearing sandals. This trait was featured in the movie.

Margot Robbie and Sharon Tate share another connection: Barbie. Robbie starred in the 2023 box-office hit, while Tate's character in *Don't Make Waves* – Malibu – is widely believed to have been the inspiration behind the 1971 Malibu Barbie. As well as being physically beautiful enough to have inspired a Barbie doll, Sharon was beautiful on the inside, too. She was described by friend and co-star Mia Farrow as 'as sweet and pure a human being as I have ever known', while Patty Duke called her 'a gentle, gentle creature', adding, 'I was crazy about her, and I didn't know anyone who wasn't.' More than 200 people attended Sharon's funeral, which was held at Holy Cross Memorial Park in Culver City, California. She was buried with her unborn son in her arms, who was named Paul Richard posthumously, in honour of his two grandfathers.

Polanski was away in London at the time of his wife's death and, on receiving the devastating news, is said to have 'disintegrated'. He became obsessed with trying to discover who had committed the crime and briefly suspected Hollywood star Bruce Lee, who was his friend and personal kung fu instructor, due to a pair of horn-rimmed glasses found at the scene. He soon realized that Lee had nothing to do with the horrifying murders. In the 2014 book *Sharon Tate: Recollection* by Debra Tate, he talks of his grief. 'Even after so many years, I find myself unable to watch a spectacular sunset or visit a lovely old house… without instinctively telling myself how much she would have loved it all. In these ways I shall remain faithful to her till the day I die.'

Paul Walker

Age of death: 40

Date of Death: 30 November 2013

Cause of death: Car accident

'The dream is to have it all... You only live one time – I want to get it all in.'

His Life

They say life begins at 40. For Paul Walker, tragically, this is when his life came to an abrupt end. He had previously stated that when he reached this age, he would reassess his life, perhaps stop acting and try something different. But it was his daughter Meadow Rain – who moved away from her mother in Hawaii to live with her dad in California at the age of 13 – who had persuaded him to stick with the big screen. She wanted him to continue acting so she could travel the world with him. 'Would that be so bad?' Walker had asked. It likely would have been great. But fate had other plans.

Having been a key part of one of the most successful movie franchises of all time – *The Fast and the Furious* franchise has made eleven movies, plus a handful of spin-off films, amassing more than $7 billion at the global box office – there's no denying that Paul Walker was, primarily, an action hero. His parts in *Takers*, *Bobby Z, Vehicle 19* and *Into the Blue* confirm his gutsy credentials. But he also had range, playing more varied roles, from the picture-perfect jock in *Pleasantville* to a frantic father in *Hours*, to a World War II soldier in *Flags of Our Fathers*, and an Antarctic dog-sled guide in Disney's *Below Eight*. Oh, and kind of a douchebag in *She's All That*. Walker did have the opportunity to play the ultimate hero: Superman. But when he was offered the part for the 2006 *Superman Returns*, he turned it down. Why? Some say it's because he didn't want to become afflicted with the 'Superman curse' – a series of misfortunes that have struck various people working on Superman films and TV shows. Among those said to have been 'cursed' due to their Superman association include: Christopher Reeve, George Reeves, Richard Pryor, Marlon Brando, Margot Kidder and Gene Hackman.

Although Walker appeared in more than thirty movies and ten television series, including *The Young and the Restless* (for which he was nominated in the Outstanding Male Newcomer category in the Soap Opera Digest Awards in 1994), acting wasn't his biggest passion. Cars were a huge part of Walker's life. A self-confessed gearhead and adrenaline junkie, Walker would race fast cars and competed semi-professionally in the Redline Time Attack series. He was accomplished enough to perform some of his own *Fast and Furious* stunts, and admitted that he was probably 'the illegal U-turn king of LA'. Indeed, he had his driving licence suspended for making too many illegal U-turns and racking up too many speeding tickets… although this didn't stop him from getting behind the wheel. He had a collection of around thirty vehicles, including Audis, BMWs, Ferraris, Porsches, a Rolls-Royce and the natty Nissan Skyline GT-R R34 that he drove in *2 Fast 2 Furious*, and kept after filming wrapped. Following Walker's death, in January 2020, twenty-one of his cars, trucks and motorcycles were sold at auction, raising $2.33 million.

Although cars were a passion for Walker, they couldn't top the ocean, and he'd surf any chance he got. For him, the rest of the world disappeared when he was on a wave. But it wasn't just the *top* of the ocean that got him excited; he had a fascination with what lurks beneath, too. He cited French oceanographer, conservationist and filmmaker Jacques Cousteau (who won an Oscar for his 1956 documentary *The Silent World*, one of the first films to use underwater cinematography) as his role model and idol, deeply admiring his commitment to understanding the sea. Having majored in marine biology in community college, Walker had intended to pursue it as a career, before acting opportunities sidetracked him. In 2006, Walker became a board member of The Billfish Foundation, an organization dedicated to conserving ocean health around the world. In 2010, he spent eleven days off the coast of Mexico tagging great white sharks for National Geographic's series *Expedition Great White*. He loved the mystery of the ocean, how weird and wonderful creatures were always being found. He mused that, although we think we know a lot, all of these new discoveries are a reminder of how little we actually do know. The 2005 action-thriller *Into the Blue*, which Walker starred in with Jessica Alba (and his real-life pet dog, a Chesapeake Bay Retriever named Boone), allowed the actor to satisfy his water-baby tendencies, with much of the shoot taking place in the sea. The film didn't make much of a splash at the box office or with critics, but audiences had no complaints that they got to watch a shirtless Walker for a considerable chunk of the movie.

Which brings us to his appearance. Blond-haired, blue-eyed, 6 ft 3 in, tanned, chiselled features, six-pack, surfer-dude vibe… Walker was a handsome guy.

His good looks thrust him into the limelight at the age of 2, when he got his first modelling gig for a Pampers commercial. Fast-forward a few decades and he's making *Glamour*'s 50 Sexiest Men and *People*'s 50 Most Beautiful People lists. When he appeared on *The Ellen DeGeneres Show*, Ellen joked, 'When we book you, we have to add three extra minutes for screaming because it happens every time you come on,' which was met with a surge of screams by the largely female audience. His *Fast and Furious* co-star Tyrese Gibson said of Walker, 'Some dudes, where they're handsome and they become arrogant with it and they're unapproachable... He wasn't intimidating because he was so regular and so grounded and so cool.'

As well as being regular, grounded and cool, Walker was also kind. He once bought a $9,000 engagement ring for a couple he didn't even know when he overheard they couldn't afford it. He also set up the non-profit organization Reach Out Worldwide (ROWW) in response to the earthquake that devastated Haiti in 2010, and travelled to a number of disaster-stricken areas to offer aid. 'I'm a doer, and whether it was the tsunami in Sri Lanka or the earthquake in Indonesia, I was always saying, "I should be there; I should be helping out".'

His Death

On 30 November 2013, at around 3.30 pm, Paul Walker left a charitable event for ROWW in Santa Clarita in California and got into the passenger seat of his good friend Roger Rodas's Porsche Carrera GT. Whilst driving at around 90 mph in a 45 mph zone, the car crashed into a lamppost and two trees, then exploded. The two friends died almost instantly. The curve on Kelly Johnson Parkway is a popular spot for 'drifting', a thrilling manoeuvre where the driver intentionally oversteers. No alcohol or drugs were in either man's system, no mechanical fault was found with the car and the road conditions didn't play a part in the crash. The investigation concluded that the speed the car was travelling and the age of the tyres were the primary reasons for the accident. Walker lived, worked and died in the fast lane.

A public memorial was attended by around 6,000 people at the site of the crash, where fans and friends laid gifts, flowers, candles, notes, teddies, photos and DVDs of *The Fast and Furious* movies, before taking part in a motor procession and revving their engines to honour the star. Walker was cremated and his ashes buried at Forest Lawn Memorial Park in the Hollywood Hills during a private ceremony for close friends and family.

Walker was part way through filming *Fast & Furious 7* when he died. In order to complete the movie, repurposed old footage of Walker was combined with new scenes shot with his brothers Caleb and Cody as stand-ins (complete with fake tattoos), whose faces were later replaced with CGI versions of Paul's. The film is dedicated to Walker and some of the scenes are eerily ominous, given his passing. Like the funeral scene that sees Roman (Tyrese Gibson) saying to Walker's character Brian, 'Promise me bro, no more funerals,' to which Brian replies, 'Just one more.'

Three more films starring Walker were released after his death: *Hours*, *Brick Mansions* and *Pawn Shop Chronicles*. Walker won some awards after his death, too, including the MTV Movie Award for Best On-Screen Duo (with Vin Diesel) for *Fast & Furious 6* in 2014 and the Teen Choice Award for Choice Movie Actor: Action in 2015, for *Fast & Furious 7*. When Vin Diesel accepted awards at the 2016 People's Choice Awards for *Fast & Furious 7*, he honoured his friend by singing a couple of lines from 'See You Again', the song played over the final scene of the film. Walker's mother described Vin Diesel as her son's 'other half'. After Walker passed, Diesel posted a photo on Instagram of him and Walker with the message, 'Brother I will miss you very much. I am absolutely speechless.' In remembrance of his friend, Diesel named his daughter Pauline. Diesel is godfather to Walker's daughter Meadow, who was 15 when her father died, and who is continuing her dad's charity work through The Paul Walker Foundation, which she launched on what would have been his forty-second birthday. The foundation aims to simply 'do good' by fulfilling Paul's legacy via 'his passion for the ocean, his passion for rescuing animals, his passion for helping people and his passion for spontaneous goodwill'.

Walker's legacy also lives on through ROWW, which was taken over by his brother Cody. Paul was honoured at the Noble Awards 2015 for his humanitarian work, with Cody collecting the award, and Walker's *Fast & Furious* co-stars Tyrese Gibson and Michelle Rodriguez offering touching tributes to their dear, departed friend. Gibson said, 'Paul lived in Santa Barbara. When something happened in the Philippines, he jumps off of his surfboard… and he's on a plane to the other side of the world, to do any means necessary to make a difference.' Rodriguez told the tearful audience that Walker 'just *loves*' and described his heart as 'so open and full of wanting to give'. His death deeply affected those involved with ROWW. JD Dorfman, the organization's operations manager, released a statement after Walker died, saying: 'Some people play a hero, Paul was a hero. Paul was an honourable, hardworking, dedicated, respectful man with a humble spirit… As the ROWW family mourns the loss of our founder, leader, brother and friend, we pledge to carry out his dream of helping those when they need it most.'

Robin Williams

Age of death: 63
Date of death: 11 August 2014
Cause of death: Suicide

'Death is nature's way of saying, "Your table is ready".'

His Life

Carpe Diem. This is what is etched in cement next to Robin Williams's hand- and footprints at Grauman's Chinese Theatre on the Hollywood Walk of Fame in LA. It's also the advice his character, an enthusiastic private-school English teacher, gave his students in the 1989 *Dead Poets Society*. 'Carpe Diem. Seize the day, boys,' he whispered. 'Make your lives extraordinary.'

Williams certainly heeded his own advice. His life was indeed extraordinary; he seized an Oscar nomination for Best Actor in a Leading Role for this performance in *Dead Poets Society*, as well as many other awards throughout his career, including six Golden Globes, five Grammys, two Emmys, and an Academy Award for Best Actor in a Supporting Role for *Good Will Hunting* in 1998. He also seized the opportunity to perform in around eighty-five movies, taking roles such as a radio shock jock (*Good Morning, Vietnam*), a car salesman (*Cadillac Man*), Peter Pan (*Hook*), a Scottish nanny (*Mrs Doubtfire*), a genie (*Aladdin*), an android (*Bicentennial Man*), a gay owner of a drag club (*The Birdcage*), a creepy stalker (*One Hour Photo*) and a hapless dad (*Old Dogs*). His roles were varied, and he seemed equally comfortable playing wacky and eccentric than he did sombre and reflective. Terry Gillian, who directed Williams in *The Fisher King* and *The Adventures of Baron Munchausen*, said that the actor had the ability to 'go from manic to mad to tender and vulnerable' and that he had 'the most unique mind on the planet'.

The most common role Williams played was a doctor – albeit in different forms of the profession. He was a psychologist in *Good Will Hunting*, a neurologist in *Awakenings*, a pediatrician in *What Dreams May Come*, a physician in *Patch Adams*, and a gynecologist in *Nine Months*. Sadly, the final few months of his life were spent visiting various doctors and undergoing countless tests and scans, as they tried to ascertain what was behind the actor's symptoms of memory loss, a tremor in his hand, extreme anxiety, insomnia and delusions. 'Robin was losing his mind and he was aware of it,' said his wife Susan Schneider Williams. He was diagnosed with Parkinson's disease.

Before illness engulfed him, however, Williams was a genius both on stage with his stand-up routines, and on screen with his varied performances. Voted 'least likely to succeed' in high school, he got the last laugh on his classmates… and millions of other laughs besides. His big break came in the late 1970s when he played alien Mork in the television sitcom *Mork & Mindy*. Having been the same character in an episode of *Happy Days*, Williams had entertained viewers so much that the spin-off show *Mork & Mindy* was created, transforming the quirky actor into a superstar. At its peak, the show had a weekly audience of sixty million. Williams improvised many of his lines – ad-libbing with whatever his hilarious mind threw at him – and this comedic style stayed with him throughout his career. When doing the voice for Genie in *Aladdin*, the creators had sixteen hours of material due to Williams's improvisation, with the talented impressionist mimicking dozens of celebrities, including Robert De Niro, Ed Sullivan, Groucho Marx and Arnold Schwarzenegger. Because of this improvisation, the script had to be rejected for a Best Adapted Screenplay Oscar nomination! Aladdin was the highest-grossing film in 1992, making more than $504 million at the box office worldwide.

Williams didn't get every part he went for, though. He'd put himself forward to play Hagrid in the Harry Potter films but, alas, because of the rule imposed by the producers – and J.K. Rowling herself – that all actors must be British, Williams was turned down.

From 1986 to 1998 (and again in 2006 to raise money for the Hurricane Katrina relief), Robin Williams, Billy Crystal and Whoopi Goldberg co-hosted Comic Relief USA, which has raised more than $70 million over the years. The three comics became close friends and would visit many homeless shelters around America, delivering money raised from their comedy shows. In every movie he was in, Williams had it written into his contract that the production company was to hire a certain number of people living on the streets as extras or support staff on set. It's been estimated that he helped more than 1,500 homeless people this way. Williams also took his kind heart to thirteen different countries to perform to – and lift the spirits of – around 90,000 troops on the United Service Organizations (USO) circuit. On helping people, Robin said: 'Self goes away. Ego, bye-bye. The thing that matters is others. That's what life's about.'

In the 1970s and early 1980s, Williams struggled with alcohol and cocaine addiction. He'd been with fellow comedian and friend John Belushi the night of his fatal drug overdose, which – along with the impending birth of his first child – motivated Williams to get clean. Williams stayed sober for twenty years but relapsed while on location in Alaska filming *Insomnia*. In 2006, he admitted himself into a rehab centre to battle his alcoholism, then again in mid-2014, a couple of months before his death. He often used his addiction as material in his stand-up performances, with jokes like: 'I went to rehab in wine country… to keep my options open.'

The last film that Williams starred in was *Night at the Museum: Secret of the Tomb*. Playing Theodore Roosevelt, something wasn't right on set. He struggled to remember his lines or find the right words for his performance; his confidence was low and he simply wasn't himself. Director Shawn Levy later said, 'It was clear to all of us on that set that something was going on with Robin.' The final words that Williams utters in the film – and ever on screen – are: 'Smile, my boy. It's sunrise.'

His Death

On 11 August 2014, Robin Williams committed suicide by hanging himself at his California home, at the age of 63. Neither illegal drugs nor alcohol had been in his system. Some media outlets speculated that financial troubles were at the root of the actor's decision to end his life, while others blamed his addiction demons. He was cremated at Monte's Chapel of the Hills in San Anselmo and his ashes were scattered over San Francisco Bay. Having been diagnosed with Parkinson's disease, his autopsy showed that, in fact, he had been suffering with Lewy body dementia (LBD), which would explain why he had been struggling with such intense fear, anxiety, paranoia and hallucinations. His widow, Susan, went on to write an article in the *Neurology* journal titled 'The Terrorist Inside My Husband's Brain', in which she outlined their agonizing experiences. She explained that all of the doctors she met with after her husband's death agreed that Williams had had one of the worst LBD pathologies they had ever seen; nearly every region of his brain was under attack. As Susan watched her spouse battle his unknown illness, it was devastating to see 'the bravest man in the world playing the hardest role of his life,' she said.

The 2020 documentary *Robin's Wish* explores the effects that LBD had on Robin, explaining that he fought the disease as best he could, despite not knowing what he was dealing with. Distinguished professor of neurology Bruce Miller said that he was amazed that Robin could walk or move at all, given the severity of his illness. But the documentary then states: 'People who are incredibly brilliant can tolerate degenerative diseases better. Robin Williams was a genius.' This genius was recognized by President Barack Obama after his death, when he released a statement saying: 'Robin Williams was an airman, a doctor, a genie, a nanny, a president, a professor, a bangarang, Peter Pan, and everything in between… He arrived in our lives as an alien – but he ended up touching every element of the human spirit.' Fans created makeshift memorials for the star with flowers, notes, teddy bears, candles and gifts at various locations, including his star on the Hollywood Walk of Fame; the San Francisco home featured in *Mrs Doubtfire*; the bench in Boston's Public Garden from *Good Will Hunting*; the Parrish Shoes sign in Keene, New Hampshire, where parts of *Jumanji* were filmed; and *Mork & Mindy*'s home in Boulder, Colorado.

In 2017, the Robin Williams Legacy of Laughter Award was established through the charity Bring Change to Mind, founded by Glenn Close, which aims to end the stigma associated with mental illness. Williams's three children Zak, Zelda and Cody have presented the award to Billy Crystal, Whoopi Goldberg, Ben Stiller and Will Smith. 'Our family is being honored from one Genie family to another,' said Smith, making reference to the fact that both he and Williams played Genie in different versions of *Aladdin*. Robin was honoured in CeeLo Green's song 'Robin Williams', which also mentions his peers who died before their time too, such as John Belushi, Richard Pryor, Philip Seymour Hoffman, Chris Farley, Bernie Mac and Phil Hartman.

During the opening of International Youth Day: Mental Health Matters on 12 August 2014, held at the United Nations headquarters, Assistant Secretary General Thomas Gass paid tribute to Williams by standing on the desk – just as his character Mr Keating had done in *Dead Poets Society* – and quoting his line: 'Dare to look at things in a different way'. Several fans – including TV host Jimmy Fallon – paid homage to Williams with video reenactments of the emotional 'O captain! My captain!' scene, which sees the characters standing on their desks in solidarity with their mentor.

The city of San Francisco, which Williams called home, has honoured its late, great resident in its own way. A mural of him on Market Street, which highlights his gentle, blue eyes, was painted in 2018. Another popped up in the Bay Area in 2021. The tunnel with a rainbow painted over its arch on Highway 101 is now called the Robin Williams Tunnel. And the Sharon Meadow in Golden Gate Park, where the annual Comedy Day is held, has been renamed the Robin Williams Meadow. An asteroid has also been named after him – the 12820 Robinwilliams. How fitting that, during the Emmy Awards tribute speech about his good friend, Billy Crystal said, 'For almost forty years, he was the brightest star in a comedy galaxy.'

Natalie Wood

Age of death: 43

Date of death: 29 November 1981

Cause of death: Drowning and other undetermined factors

'I'm just going to have to grow old
because I'm too terrified to have anything done.'

Her Life

Which eight-year-old wouldn't want to star in a movie alongside Santa? That's just what the cute, precocious Natalie Wood thought she was doing when she played Susan Walker in the 1947 *Miracle on 34th Street*. 'I really did think that Edmund Gwenn was Santa,' the actress said many years later, as she had never seen him without his beard. After the popularity of the film, Wood was counted among the top Hollywood child stars – alongside Shirley Temple and Elizabeth Taylor – and was invited to appear in the Macy's annual Thanksgiving Parade (which was featured in the movie). Little Susan in *Miracle on 34th Street* wasn't the childhood star's first role, though: the camera began loving her at the age of 4, when she made a fifteen-second appearance alongside her mother in *Happy Land*, being credited as 'Little Girl Who Drops Ice Cream Cone'.

In the fifty-plus movies that Wood appeared in throughout her career (around twenty of which she made as a child), her characters actually had names. Memorable ones being Helen Gurley Brown in *Sex and the Single Girl*, Louise Hovick in *Gypsy* and Judy in *Rebel Without a Cause*. She landed an Oscar nomination for the latter film, as Best Actress in a Supporting Role. Her other two Oscar nominations were for Best Actress in a Leading Role, for 1961's *Splendor in the Grass* and 1963's *Love with the Proper Stranger*. The star's real name was Natalia Zakharenko, but movie executives changed the Russian-American's name to Natalie Wood, as a tribute to filmmaker Sam Wood, to make it more agreeable to English-speaking audiences.

Arguably her best role was as Maria in *West Side Story*, despite the fact that it wasn't actually *her* singing in the movie. Marni Nixon is now recognized as the singing voice of actresses in several musicals, including Audrey Hepburn in *My Fair Lady*, Deborah Kerr in *The King and I* and, indeed, Natalie Wood in *West Side Story*. But when the films were released, audiences were none the wiser. Wood did sing in *Gypsy*, however. Throughout the 1960s, Wood was one of the biggest Hollywood stars around, along with the likes of Audrey Hepburn and Sophia Loren. Director Sydney Pollack, who directed Wood in *This Property is Condemned*, said of her: 'When she was right for the part, there was no one better. She was a damn good actress.' In this film, she had to appear in a scene where she was standing in a steel water tank for cattle. She was so afraid of dark water that co-star Robert Blake had to dive under the water, holding his breath, to steady her legs so she could perform.

Another Robert – Robert Redford – also starred alongside Wood in *This Property is Condemned*, and was just one of her many love interests on screen. James Dean, Steve McQueen, Gene Kelly, Tony Curtis and Richard Beymer – to name a few – all had the pleasure of kissing the doe-eyed beauty in the name of work. And her love life was almost as exciting in real life. Wood was linked to many famous men, including Warren Beatty (her co-star in *Splendor in the Grass*), Frank Sinatra (who she starred in *Kings Go Forth* with), Michael Caine (who co-starred in *Peeper* with her), David Niven Jr. and Elvis Presley. She also had a broken engagement with businessman Ladislav Blatnik, known as the 'Shoe King of Venezuela'.

But it wasn't all fun, romance and red carpets. In fact, some of her encounters with men were horribly sinister. She was allegedly sexually assaulted by Hollywood star Kirk Douglas when she was 16, and exploited as a teenager into a sexual entanglement with 42-year-old director Nicholas Ray to prove she could play a 'bad girl' in *Rebel Without a Cause*.

Wood got married three times – twice to the same man, Robert Wagner, who she co-starred with in *All the Fine Young Cannibals* in 1960, *The Affair* in 1973 and *Cat on a Hot Tin Roof* in 1976. They had a daughter named Courtney, a younger sister for Wood's other daughter Natasha, who she had with her second husband, film producer and screenwriter Richard Gregson. Lana Wood – who played Bond girl Plenty O'Toole in *Diamonds are Forever* – recalled when her sister announced her second engagement to Wagner at a family dinner party. She'd been perturbed when Natalie said, 'Sometimes it's better to be with the devil you know than the devil you don't.' In *Natalie Wood: The Complete Biography*, author Suzanne Finstad writes about the demise of Wagner and Wood's first marriage – when Wood caught her husband in flagrante with their male butler. Fleeing to her parents' home that night, sobbing and bleeding from a crystal glass she'd smashed in her hand, Wood shut herself in a bedroom and accidentally overdosed on sleeping pills. She was rushed to hospital, where her stomach was pumped. This wasn't the only time that Wood brought harm on herself. After her split from Warren Beatty in 1963, she is reported to have taken 'enough sleeping pills to kill herself'. Wood described their two-year relationship as a 'collision' from beginning to end.

Natalie Wood's career took her from childhood star to teenage ingénue to an alluring starlet who dazzled audiences with her beauty, voice and talent – her style dubbed by critics as 'luminous' and 'intimate'. From the start of her career to the end, she was praised and admired. Aged 9, she was cited in *Parents* magazine as the 'most exciting juvenile motion picture star of the year', and described by *Tomorrow is Forever* co-star Orson Welles as 'so good, she was terrifying'. In one of her last interviews before her death, Wood was described as 'our sexual conscience on the silver screen', and *Life* said she had a 'dark fresh loveliness'. Certainly, Natalie Wood had come a long way from the 'Little Girl Who Drops Ice Cream Cone'.

Her Death

The circumstances surrounding Natalie Wood's death on 29 November 1981 remain a mystery to this day. Initially, after her body – dressed in a nightgown and red parka – was discovered floating in the water a little before 8 am just off California's Catalina Island, it was declared an accidental drowning. She had been aboard her fifty-five-foot yacht the *Splendour*, along with her husband Robert Wagner, co-star in *Brainstorm* Christopher Walken, and the boat's captain Dennis Davern. Wagner, Walken and Davern told police the same story about the night Natalie died: she must have taken the dinghy out by herself and gotten into trouble in the icy waters. It wasn't until three decades later that Davern changed his story. He said that, following a smashed bottle of wine and accusation from Wagner to Walken – 'What are you trying to do, fuck my wife?' – Wagner and Wood had an 'ugly' argument. Fuelled by alcohol and jealousy, it sounded to Davern like there was a physical fight. Then, all of a sudden… eerie silence. Wagner told Davern that his wife was 'gone', suggesting that she took the dinghy ashore, then discouraged Davern from contacting the coastguard – instead inviting him to drink scotch with him. Around three hours later, the coastguard was finally contacted. Davern, Natalie's sister Lana and detectives working the case have since said that Wood taking the dinghy is a highly unlikely scenario given it was dark, cold, the sea was rough and Natalie was afraid of the water. 'I've always been terrified of water, dark water, sea water,' she'd previously said.

Two weeks after the 43-year-old actress's death, the case was officially closed but, thirty years later, in 2011, it was reopened due to new evidence and witness statements, including Davern's. Two other witnesses from a nearby boat said they had heard a woman scream for help. The bruises found on Wood's body and arms – plus abrasions on the left side of her face – suggested she'd been assaulted before her death. Lana believes her sister was pushed from the boat by Wagner but he maintains his innocence.

Ultimately, while foul play is suspected, there's not enough evidence to say one way or the other what actually happened. The cause of death was changed from 'accidental drowning' to 'drowning and other undetermined factors', and detective Ralph Hernandez said, 'We have not been able to prove that this was a homicide, and we have not been able to prove that this was an accident, either. The ultimate problem is, we don't know how she ended up in the water.'

Wood was buried in Westwood Village Memorial Park Cemetery in Los Angeles. International press, photographers and members of the public tried to attend her funeral but were not allowed in; they had to remain outside the cemetery walls. Her coffin was covered with 1,000 gardenias and carried by Frank Sinatra, Rock Hudson, Laurence Olivier, Gregory Peck, David Niven, Fred Astaire and movie director Elia Kazan. Other members of the Hollywood elite attending the funeral included Elizabeth Taylor, Gene Kelly, Stephanie Powers and Christopher Walken.

'My mom loved gardenias, so whenever I smell them, I always think of my mom,' said her daughter Natasha, who, along with her half-sister Courtney, launched the perfume 'Natalie' in their mother's honour in 2015. The fragrance uses gardenia as one of the key notes. Another way the women – who lost their mother when they were 7 and 11 – keep Natalie's memory alive is by partnering with CoachArt, an organization that teaches athletics and art to chronically ill children. Part of the sales from their fragrance is donated to CoachArt. They remember that their mother would read them Russian fairy tales at bedtime and filled their lives with fun.

Natalie's legacy also lives on on the Hollywood Walk of Fame, where she was posthumously inducted in 1984. This was the year after her final film, *Brainstorm*, was released. Following her sudden death, the ending of the film had to be rewritten and her character was written out of at least three scenes, with soundalikes and a stand-in being used to replace the star in some of her key shots. The closing credits of the movie include a dedication to Wood, saying simply 'To Natalie'.

Bibliography

John Belushi

Belushi, Jim – 'There's an old saying: "When you drink the water, remember the men and women who dug the well". John dug the well for me… When my brother passed, Dan Aykroyd and John Candy just swooped in on me and they put their wings around me and healed me with love and attention.' 'Jim Belushi Gets Emotional Remembering Late Brother John Belushi', KFC Radio, uploaded to YouTube January 2022, www.youtube.com/watch?v=kLKLLiX7MTo

Belushi, John –'In your twenties, you feel like you're indestructible… In your thirties, you think "I'll be around here a little longer, so I'm going to take better care of myself".' 'John Belushi: More Than a Pretty Face' (by Lewis Grossberger), *Rolling Stone*, January 1982, www.rollingstone.com/tv-movies/tv-movie-features/john-belushi-saturday-night-live-more-than-a-pretty-face-98538

Belushi, John – 'I'd rather be an anarchist than a professional.' *Belushi* (directed by R. J. Cutler), Passion Pictures, Showtime Networks, Sky Atlantic, This Machine Filmworks, 2020

Helm, Nick – 'You had this well-rounded cast and then you had this one guy who cut through everyone, and that was Belushi. Like Animal from The Muppets, he was everyone's favourite.' *Belushi* (directed by R. J. Cutler), Passion Pictures, Showtime Networks, Sky Atlantic, This Machine Filmworks, 2020

Jacklin, Judy – 'He went from zero to 100 so quickly, and that surprised people.' '"He was a Radical": John Belushi Remembered by His Wife and Fellow Comics' (by Brian Logan), *The Guardian*, November 2020, www.theguardian.com/stage/2020/nov/24/he-was-a-radical-john-belushi-remembered-by-his-wife-and-fellow-comics

Landis, John – 'It was terrible. He went from being this really sweet guy to someone hyper and maniacal.' 'John Belushi: The "Awful Addiction" that Killed Blues Brothers actor (by Lauren Russell), *Express*, August 2022, www.express.co.uk/life-style/health/1658415/john-belushi-blues-brothers-drug-addiction-cocaine-heroin-symptoms

Robert De Niro and Robin Williams taking drugs with John Belushi the night he died. *The Castle on Sunset* (by Shawn Levy), Weidenfeld & Nicolson, 2019

Williams, Robin – 'Here's this guy who's a beast, who could do anything, and he's gone. That sobered the shit out of me.' *Robin Williams: Come Inside My Mind* (directed by Marina Zenovich), HBO Documentary Films, Jigsaw Productions, 2018

Chadwick Boseman

Boseman, Chadwick – 'You have to cherish things in a different way when you know the clock is ticking, you are under pressure.' Originally from an article in *The New York Times*, 2018; cited from 'Chadwick Boseman's Words of Wisdom That Still Speak to Us Five Years After His Death' (by Shanelle Genai), The Root, August 2025, www.theroot.com/chadwick-bosemans-words-of-wisdom-that-still-speak-to-u-2000059073/slides/2

Boseman, Chadwick – 'People don't make $140 million movies starring Black and brown people.' 'Chadwick Boseman on His Steph Curry Love and the *Gods of Egypt* Controversy' (by Sarah Ball), *GQ*, December 2015, www.gq.com/story/chadwick-boseman-gods-of-egypt

Boseman, Chadwick – 'For me, doing this, it has to be meaningful.' 'The "Black Panther" Revolution' (by Josh Eells), *Rolling Stone*, February 2018, www.rollingstone.com/tv-movies/tv-movie-features/the-black-panther-revolution-199536

Hamilton, Lewis – 'As a young Black boy, I didn't have a superhero who I could look up to who was the same colour as me… This superhero shows all these young kids that it's possible… Wakanda Forever.' 'REACTION! Lewis Hamilton Dedicates his 93rd Pole to Chadwick Boseman', Sky Sports F1, uploaded to YouTube August 2020, www.youtube.com/watch?v=Qiz9izOyh3w

'He leaves the film-making landscape looking very different to how it was when he entered it… Chadwick Boseman began his career playing African

American icons and pioneers; he ends it as one himself.' 'The Man with a Manifesto: How Chadwick Boseman Changed Film For Ever' (by Steve Rose), *The Guardian*, August 2020, www.theguardian.com/film/2020/aug/29/the-man-with-a-manifesto-how-chadwick-boseman-changed-film-forever

Rashad, Phylicia – 'What I saw in him was the sky was the limit.' 'The "Black Panther" Revolution' (by Josh Eells), *Rolling Stone*, February 2018, www.rollingstone.com/tv-movies/tv-movie-features/the-black-panther-revolution-199536

Rashad, Phylicia – 'Lanky young man with big eyes and an endearing smile.' '"One of the Greatest Actors Ever": Phylicia Rashad Remembers Her Student Chadwick Boseman' (by Charles Holmes), *Rolling Stone*, September 2020, www.rollingstone.com/tv-movies/tv-movie-features/phylicia-rashad-chadwick-boseman-in-her-own-words-105376

Smith, Shawn – 'Chadwick Boseman's legacy has paved the way for me. He showed that you aren't just limited to these basic roles; you can do whatever you want.' 'Chadwick Boseman's Widow Breaks Her Silence in Exclusive 1st Interview, *Good Morning America'*, uploaded to YouTube November 2022, www.youtube.com/watch?v=rPV8TRb_rQc

The BBC described Boseman as 'a film icon who changed Hollywood'. 'Chadwick Boseman: A Film Icon Who Changed Hollywood' (by Hanna Flint), BBC Culture, December 2020, www.bbc.co.uk/culture/article/20201214-chadwick-boseman-a-film-icon-who-changed-hollywood

John Candy

Candy, John – 'I think I may have become an actor to hide from myself. You can escape into a character.' 'John Candy' (by Biography Editors), Biography, May 2021, www.biography.com/actors/john-candy

Candy, Christopher – 'Whenever I feel like I lose the importance of him to people, I just remember that happened.' 'John Candy Remembered: His Children Share New Stories About Their Late Father On the Eve of His Birthday' (by Ryan Parker), *The Hollywood Reporter*, October 2016, www.hollywoodreporter.com/movies/movie-features/john-candy-remembered-his-children-939218

Candy, Jennifer – 'He worked so hard on that... He had a dialect coach... He was so worried about it, getting that accent down.' 'John Candy

Remembered: His Children Share New Stories About Their Late Father On the Eve of His Birthday' (by Ryan Parker), *The Hollywood Reporter*, October 2016, www.hollywoodreporter.com/movies/movie-features/john-candy-remembered-his-children-939218

Columbus, Chris – 'The funeral-parlour story, that was all improvised at 4:30 in the morning... We could barely keep a straight face on set just listening to John.' '"Home Alone" at 30: Director Chris Columbus Talks Trump "Bullying His Way" into a Cameo and More Never-Before-Told Stories' (by Jason Guerrasio), *Business Insider*, December 2020, www.businessinsider.com/home-alone-30-anniversary-chris-columbus-trump-cameo-2020-11

Martin, Steve – 'He was a very sweet guy. Very sweet and complicated. He was always friendly, always outgoing and funny and nice and polite but I could tell he had kind of a little broken heart inside of him.' 'JC Corcoran – Steve Martin Interview', *News 4*, uploaded to YouTube March 2014, www.youtube.com/watch?v=DOPlluuulVY

O'Hara, Catherine – Referring to Candy as the 'patron saint of laughter', she called him 'bright and quick and graceful and full of ideas', and said his movies were 'a safe haven for those of us who get overwhelmed by the sadness and troubles of this world.' She added, 'He left us a library of fun to remember him by.' 'John Candy's Memorial Service', originally broadcast on ITV Canada, March 1994; uploaded to YouTube by Crossing the Themes, June 2020, www.youtube.com/watch?v=vg9vtVygn8Y

Ween, Gene – 'There was so much going on about Kurt Cobain and nobody mentioned John Candy at all. I have a special little spot in my heart for him.' 'The Goofy Duo Serves Up "Chocolate and Cheese" on Their Latest Effort' (by Chuck Dean), *Rolling Stone*, April 1995, www.rollingstone.com/music/music-news/qa-ween-70387

James Dean

Bogart, Humphrey – 'Dean died at just the right time. He left behind a legend. If he had lived, he'd never have been able to live up to his publicity.' *Bogart* (by Richard Gehman), Fawcett, 1965

Dean, James – 'Live fast, die young, leave a good-looking corpse.' *Knock on Any Door* (by Willard Motley), Collins, January 1948

Dean, James – 'No, I am not a homosexual. But I'm also not going to go through life with one hand tied behind my back.' *The Unabridged James Dean: His Life and Legacy from A to Z* (by Randall Riese), McGraw-Hill/Contemporary, 1991

Dean, James – 'The life you might save might be *mine.*' 'James Dean – Driving PSA', uploaded to YouTube by jamisano, April 2007, www.youtube.com/watch?v=hU5N2SrEaZI

Ernst, Anton – 'We do not intend to let his fans down.' 'Director of New James Dean Movie Speaks Out Over Backlash to Star's "Casting"' (by Sharareh Drury), *The Hollywood Reporter*, November 2019, www.hollywoodreporter.com/news/general-news/director-new-james-dean-movie-speaks-backlash-stars-casting-1253232

Presley, Elvis – 'We're sullen, we're broodin', we're something of a menace… That's what the girls like in men… I know you can't be sexy if you smile. You can't be a rebel if you grin.' Originally from an article in *Parade* (by Lloyd Shearer), 1956; cited from *Last Train to Memphis: The Rise of Elvis Presley* (by Peter Guralnick), Abacus, November 1995

Taylor, Elizabeth – 'He hadn't made up his mind. He was only 24 when he died… He flirted around.' Originally from an article in *POZ* (by Kevin Sessums), November, 1997; cited from 'AIDS: Elizabeth Taylor Tells the Truth' (by *Windy City* Staff), *Windy City Times*, April 2011, www.windycitytimes.com/2011/04/27/aids-elizabeth-taylor-tells-the-truth

'What is essential is invisible to the eye.' *The Little Prince* (by Antoine de Saint-Exupéry), Reynal & Hitchcock, 1943

Carrie Fisher

Fisher, Carrie – 'No matter how I go, I want it reported that I drowned in moonlight, strangled by my own bra.' / 'I feel I'm very sane about how crazy I am.' *Wishful Drinking* (by Carrie Fisher), Simon & Schuster, 2009

Fisher, Carrie – 'I hope I slept with you to get the job, because if not, who the hell was that guy?' / 'There's no underwear in space.' 'Carrie Fisher Roasts George Lucas at AFI Life Achievement Award', American

Film Institute, uploaded to YouTube February 2009, www.youtube.com/watch?v=lZ97s396kb0

Fisher, Carrie – '[Electroconvulsive therapy treatments] blow apart the cement in [my] brain.' *The Oprah Winfrey Show*, Harpo Studios, HBO Films, HD Vision Studios, High Noon Productions, February 2011

Fisher, Carrie – Drugs made her feel more normal and 'contained' her. 'Interview: The Fisher Queen' (by Lybi Ma), *Psychology Today*, November 2001, www.psychologytoday.com/us/articles/200111/interview-the-fisher-queen

Fisher, Carrie – 'Princess Leia will be on my tombstone.' '20 Questions for Carrie Fisher' (by Lauren Paige Kennedy), *WebMD*, November 2010, www.webmd.com/mental-health/addiction/features/questions-for-carrie-fisher

Fisher, Todd – 'My family, in particular, could overwhelm most people.' *Bright Lights: Starring Carrie Fisher and Debbie Reynolds* (directed by Alexis Bloom and Fisher Stevens), Bloomfish Pictures, HBO Documentary Films, Insurgent Docs, RatPac Documentary Films, 2016

Fisher, Todd – 'I miss her so much. I want to be with Carrie.' 'Debbie Reynolds Last Words… "I Want to Be with Carrie"' (by TMZ Staff), TMZ, December 2016, www.tmz.com/2016/12/28/debbie-reynolds-tmz-000

Fisher, Todd – 'She loved it. Billie and I felt it was where she'd want to be.' 'Carrie Fisher's Giant Prozac Pill Urn Explained by Brother Todd After Debbie Reynolds' Funeral' (by Alex Ungerman), *Entertainment Tonight*, January 2017, www.etonline.com/news/206655_carrie_fisher_giant_prozac_pill_urn_explained_by_brother_todd_after_debbie_reynold_funeral

Fry, Stephen – 'She's on the edge of sanity… Not mad enough to be committed but not sane enough to lead much of a normal life.' *Stephen Fry: The Secret Life of the Manic Depressive* (directed by Ross Wilson), IWC Media, 2006

Lourd, Billie – Said that her mother was 'glitter' and 'covered the world in it, both literally and metaphorically.' / 'She left a mark of her sparkle on everyone she met.' 'Carrie Fisher: Star Wars Day Walk of Fame Honour Overshadowed by Family Row' (by Ian Youngs), BBC News, May 2023, www.bbc.co.uk/news/entertainment-arts-65480084

Clark Gable

Crawford, Joan – 'He was a king wherever he went. He earned the title. He walked like one, he behaved like one, and he was the most masculine male that I have ever met in my life… Gable had balls.' *The David Frost Show*, Group W Productions, January 1970

Day, Doris – 'He was as masculine as any man I've ever known, and as much a little boy as a grown man could be – it was this combination that had such a devastating effect on women.' *Clark Gable: A Biography* (by Warren G. Harris), Aurum Press, 2003

Eisenhower, Dwight D. – 'Be a good boy, Clark, and do as the doctors tell you to do.' *The Hollywood Book of Death* (by James Robert Parish), McGraw-Hill, October 2001

Gable, Clark – 'Hell, if I'd jumped on all the dames I'm supposed to have jumped on, I'd have had no time to go fishing.' 'The Tormented Star' (by Neil Norman), *Express*, March 2010, www.express.co.uk/expressyourself/161649/The-tormented-star

Gable, Clark – [It's] 'pure bullshit... I'm just a lucky slob from Ohio.' 'Happy Birthday, Clark Gable', Dear Mr Gable, February 2015, www.dearmrgable.com/?p=10120

Gable, Clark – 'On my tombstone they should write, "He was lucky and he knew it".' Originally from 'Gable: Last Look at a King' (by Stanley Gordon), *Look*, January 1961; cited from Dear Mr Gable, www.dearmrgable.com/?page_id=3662

Gable, Clark – He described his marriage to the actress as 'a perfect thing'. Originally from an article in *Modern Screen*, 1948; cited from 'Which Girl Has the Gable?', Dear Mr Gable, www.dearmrgable.com/?page_id=3259

Gable, Clark – 'You can trust that little screwball with your life.' *Gable & Lombard: A Biography* (by Warren G. Harris), Graymalkin Media, 2016

Gable, Clark – 'She damn near gave me a heart attack!' *The Hollywood Book of Death* (by James Robert Parish), McGraw-Hill, October 2001

Hughes, Howard – Gable's ears made him look like 'a taxicab with both doors open'. *The Celluloid Muse: Hollywood Directors Speak* (by Charles Higham and Joel Greenberg), Angus & Robertson, 1969

Zanuck, Darryl F. – 'His ears are too big and he looks like an ape.' *Leading Men: The 50 Most Unforgettable Actors of the Studio Era* (by Frank Miller), Chronicle Books, 2006

James Gandolfini

Bracco, Lorraine – 'He gave me this lovely *cock*.' *James Gandolfini: Tribute to a Friend* (directed by John Kelleher), HBO, 2013

Chase, David – '[Gandolfini was] almost a hippy.' 'David Chase Talks Working With James Gandolfini And The Sopranos Dialogue Secret', *George Stroumboulopoulos Tonight*, CBC, uploaded to YouTube by Strombo, December 2012, www.youtube.com/watch?v=zkKO6l87y3o

Chase, David – 'I also feel you're my brother because of the things we both loved. Family. Work. People in all their imperfection. Food. Alcohol. Talking. Rage... We amused each other.' '"Sopranos"' Creator David Chase's Eulogy for James Gandolfini (by *Variety* Staff), *Variety*, June 2013, www.variety.com/2013/tv/news/james-gandolfini-funeral-read-sopranos-creator-david-chases-eulogy-1200502711

Chianese, Dominic – 'There are few like Jimmy – he was homemade wine: honest, good, pure, nothing added... Loyalty and truthfulness, that was him.' *James Gandolfini: Tribute to a Friend* (directed by John Kelleher), HBO, 2013

Gandolfini, James – 'I like dark places.' 'Once Tough Guy, Now Nurturer' (by Melena Ryzik), Houma Today, www.houmatoday.com/story/news/2010/10/31/once-tough-guy-now-nurturer/26945495007/

Gandolfini, James – 'Take over for a while, I'll be right back.' / **'[Tony's weight] actually is important... When I do get thin... I don't feel the same, I don't walk the same... You know, with that lumber.'** *Inside the Actors Studio* with James Lipton (directed by Jeff Wurtz), Ovation, The Actors Studio, Triage Entertainment, Betelgeuse Productions LLC, Bravo Cable, In the Moment Productions Ltd., October 2004

'Gandolfini the great.' 'Review: *The Drop*: Bane and Lehane in a Brooklyn Thriller' (by Richard Corliss), *Time*, September 2014, www.time.com/3338255/the-drop-movie-review

Judy Garland

Bolger, Ray – 'Judy… just plain wore out.' 'Singers: End of the Rainbow', *Time*, July 1969, www.time.com/archive/6634286/singers-end-of-the-rainbow

Garland, Judy – 'I believe in the idea of the rainbow. And I've spent my entire life trying to get over it.' 'Over The Rainbow With Judy Garland: Her Best Quotes', *Marie Claire*, June 2015, www.marieclaire.co.uk/entertainment/people/judy-garland-best-quotes-69365

Heritage Auctions – 'Holy Grail of Hollywood memorabilia.' 'Dorothy's Ruby Slippers Sell for $28m at Auction' (by Robin Levinson King), BBC News, December 2024, www.bbc.co.uk/news/articles/crk008xemvno#

'[*Judy at Carnegie Hall* was] the greatest night in show-business history.' 'Judy Garland: The Greatest Night In Show Business History' (by Leon Nock), *Jazz Journal*, October 2022, www.jazzjournal.co.uk/2022/10/26/judy-garland-the-greatest-night-in-show-business-history

Marx, Groucho – '[This is] the biggest robbery since Brink's.' 'Judy Garland's Awards Show History: Historic Wins & Perplexing Losses' (by Paul Grein), *Billboard*, October 2022, www.billboard.com/lists/judy-garland-awards-show-history/feb-29-1940-academy-awards

Phillips, Stevie – '[Judy was] a demented, demanding, supremely talented drug addict.' *Judy & Liza & Robert & Freddie & David & Sue & Me… A Memoir* (by Stevie Phillips), St Martin's Press, 2015

Rooney, Mickey – 'She was a great talent and a great human being. She… has found that rainbow. At least I hope she has.' 'The Rainbow That Judy Garland Never Got Over', *The New York Times*, June 2016, www.nytimes.com/interactive/projects/cp/obituaries/archives/judy-garland

Corey Haim

Ebert, Roger – 'He creates one of the most three-dimensional, complicated, interesting characters of any age in any recent movie. If he can continue to act this well, he will never become a half-forgotten child star, but will continue to grow into an important actor. He is that good.' Originally from a review in *Chicago Sun-Times* (by Roger Ebert), March 1986; cited from 'Reviews: *Lucas*', RobertEbert.com, www.rogerebert.com/reviews/lucas-1986

Feldman, Corey – 'I am not going to watch him destroy himself.' 'Corey Haim: The Lost Boy' (by Josh Rottenberg), *Entertainment Weekly*, March 2010, www.ew.com/article/2010/03/19/corey-haim-lost-boy

Feldman, Corey – 'I always feared this day would come... Nobody will ever understand the brotherhood we shared... Nobody will ever know how to do the secret Corey handshake... I pray that you are safe and warm and finally filled with peace. I love you.' 'A Letter for the Grave... (An Open Letter to Corey Haim)', The Feldman Journal: The Official Corey Feldman Blog, March 2010, www.coreyfeldman.wordpress.com/2010/03/16/a-letter-for-the-grave-an-open-letter-to-corey-haim

Feldman, Corey – Paedophiles in the movie industry were 'passing us back and forth to each other.' 'Corey Feldman on Elijah Wood Hollywood Pedophilia Controversy: "I Would Love to Name Names"' (by Seth Abramovitch), *The Hollywood Reporter*, May 2016, www.hollywoodreporter.com/news/general-news/corey-feldman-elijah-wood-hollywood-897403

Feldman, Corey – 'This is a tragic loss of a wonderful, beautiful, tormented soul.' 'Corey Feldman's Tribute' (by *Cosmo* Team), *Cosmopolitan*, March 2010, www.cosmopolitan.com/uk/entertainment/news/a8557/corey-feldmans-tribute-99031

Feldman, Corey – 'Corey dedicated his life to the film industry. The same industry that failed to dedicate even 30 seconds to his memory.' 'Corey Feldman Mad About Corey Haim's Oscar Snub' (by TMZ Staff), TMZ, February 2011, www.tmz.com/2011/02/28/corey-haim-corey-feldman-oscars-in-memoriam-left-out-snubbed

Haim, Corey – 'There's nothing I can say except a person's got to go through what they've got to go through.' 'Corey Haim's Life Mirrored Pop Culture' (by James Montgomery), MTV Music News, March 2010, www.imdb.com/title/tt0103843/news

Haim, Corey – Branded himself a 'chronic relapser' with 'an addiction to pretty much everything.' *Larry King Live*, CNN, July 2007, transcripts.cnn.com/show/lkl/date/2007-07-20/segment/01

Haim, Corey – 'I want to be the guy they talk about when they talk about comebacks. I want people to learn from me, see I'm human.' 'Corey Haim Obituary' (by Ryan Gilbey), *The Guardian*, March 2010, www.theguardian.com/film/2010/mar/11/corey-haim-obituary

Haim, Judy – 'The Academy Awards and [Screen Actors Guild] Awards totally forgot about my kid. It hurts me as a mother because they didn't give him the honour and recognition that he deserved.' 'Corey Haim's Mom Opens Up About Son's Snubs, Tributes to Cory Monteith' (by John R. Kennedy), Global News, October 2013, www.globalnews.ca/news/883398/corey-haims-mom-opens-up-about-sons-snubs-tributes-to-cory-monteith

Anne Heche

Bradshaw, Peter – 'The movies never really knew what to do with Anne Heche. Her gamine beauty and quizzically sharp intelligence were not easily absorbed into the Hollywood templates.' 'Anne Heche was a Little Too Stylish and Smart for Hollywood' (by Peter Bradshaw), *The Guardian*, August 2022, www.theguardian.com/film/2022/aug/12/anne-heche-was-a-little-too-stylish-and-smart-for-hollywood

DeNiro, Robert – 'I'm very sad to hear of the tragic passing of Anne Heche. She was a wonderful actress and I enjoyed working with her tremendously in *Wag the Dog*. Sad! Sad! Sad!' 'Anne Heche Being Remembered by Robert De Niro as a "Wonderful Actress" Following Her Death' (by Miguel A. Melendez), *Entertainment Tonight*, August 2022, www.etonline.com/anne-heche-being-remembered-by-robert-de-niro-as-a-wonderful-actress-following-her-death-189055

Heche, Anne – 'My life is a life movies are made of.' 'Anne Celeste Heche Quotes' (by Rubaiyat Rahman), Medium, August 2022, www.medium.com/books-and-reviews/anne-celeste-heche-quotes-ad2f790bdfa9

Heche, Anne – '[I was] part of a revolution.' 'Actress, ANNE HECHE: Brave (1969-2022)' (by Derek Warburton), *Mr. Warburton*, August 2022, www.mrwarburtonmagazine.com/actress-anne-heche-brave

Heche, Anne – Calling Ellen a 'bitch'. 'Just the Two of Us: Anne Talks Ellen', *Better Together w/ Anne and Heather*, Straw Hut Media, June 2021, www.youtube.com/watch?v=pqnkj14bNrU

Heche, Anne – Heche said that she herself 'was raised in a very difficult family and that's part of why [she] needed to play Joyce Dahmer'. 'Anne Heche Related Her Difficult Upbringing To New Film "My Friend Dahmer"',

Megyn Kelly TODAY, NBC News, November 2017, www.youtube.com/watch?v=MYzR4De-QIM

Heche, Anne – '[I was] raised in a cult.' *Call Me Crazy* (by Anne Heche), Washington Square Press, February 2003

Heche, Anne – She wrote *Call Me Crazy* 'to say goodbye, once and for all to [her] story of shame and embrace [her] life choice of love… Happy freedom Anne. You have made it to the other side.' *Exclusive: Anne Heche Interview with Barbara Walters*, 20/20, ABC News, September 2001

Heche, Nancy – 'I am dumbfounded, in a state of shock. Doesn't Anne know what homosexuality has done to our family?' / '[There is] no place among the lies and blasphemies in the pages of this book.' 'Anne Heche's Mom, Nancy, Survives Four of Her Five Kids; Took "Poppers" and Married Lovers' (by Dana Kennedy), *New York Post*, August 2022, www.nypost.com/2022/08/13/anne-heches-mom-nancy-survives-four-of-her-five-kids/

Laffoon, Homer – 'We are convinced our mom would love the site we have chosen for her. It's beautiful, serene and she will be among her Hollywood peers.' 'Anne Heche Sons Glad She'll Be At Hollywood Forever Cemetery' (by TMZ Staff), TMZ, August 2022, www.tmz.com/2022/08/23/anne-heche-cremated-hollywood-forever-death-died-son-grateful

Maslin, Janet – 'Heche does well with what could have been [a] thankless role.' 'Film Review: *Donnie Brascoe*' (by Janet Maslin), *The New York Times*, February 1997, archive.nytimes.com/www.nytimes.com/library/film/donnie-film-review.html

Philip Seymour Hoffman

Hoffman, Philip Seymour – 'I think you should be serious about what you do because this is it. This is the only life you've got.' 'Philip Seymour Hoffman Interview – *DOUBT*' (by Steven Weintraub), Collider, December 2008, www.collider.com/philip-seymour-hoffman-interview-doubt

Hoffman, Philip Seymour – 'I didn't go out looking for negative characters; I went out looking for people who have a struggle and a fight to tackle.' 'Interrogation: Philip Seymour Hoffman' (by Meghan O'Rourke), *Slate*, January 2006, www.slate.com/news-and-politics/2006/01/an-interview-with-philip-seymour-hoffman.html

Hoffman, Philip Seymour – He described acting as 'torturous' and trying to be great as 'absolutely torturous'. / 'I was changed – permanently changed – by that experience. It was like a miracle to me.' 'A Higher Calling' (by Lynn Hirschberg), *The New York Times*, December 2008, www.nytimes.com/2008/12/21/magazine/21hoffman-t.html?pagewanted=all

Mimi O'Donnell on Philip Seymour Hoffman's relapse. 'Mimi O'Donnell Reflects on the Loss of Philip Seymour Hoffman and the Devastation of Addiction' (by Mimi O'Donnell, as told to Adam Green), *Vogue*, December 2017, www.vogue.com/article/philip-seymour-hoffman-mimi-odonnell-vogue-january-2018-issue

Minghella, Anthony – 'Philip is an extraordinary actor, cursed, sometimes, by his own gnawing intelligence… He struggles for every moment in a film, overthinks, overanalyzes, wrestles with the scene.' 'Can Philip Seymour Hoffman Do No Wrong?' (by Simon Garfield), *The Observer*, February 2006; cited from www.simongarfield.com, www.simongarfield.com/assets/pdfs/Journalism_3_some_famous_or_interesting_people/16_his_feminine_side.pdf

Whitney Houston

Costner, Kevin – 'If you could hear me now, I would tell you you weren't just good enough, you were great… You weren't just pretty, you were as beautiful as a woman could be. And people didn't just like you, Whitney. They loved you.' He encouraged Bobbi Kristina to 'sing [her] heart out'. 'Whitney Houston Funeral Coverage', CNN, February 2012, www.transcripts.cnn.com/show/se/date/2012-02-18/segment/07

Houston, Whitney – 'I'm looking forward to the years to come. Good years.' Posted on Instagram by whitneyhoustonfanclub, March 2023, www.instagram.com/p/CpO9D6lrO0M

Houston, Whitney – '[*Waiting to Exhale* is] a breakthrough for the image of Black women because it presents them both as professionals and as caring mothers.' 'No Miss Prissy' (by Christopher John Farley), *Time*, December 1995, www.web.archive.org/web/20080528223545/http://www.time.com/time/magazine/article/0,9171,983795-2,00.html

Houston, Whitney – 'Music is not a colour to me. It's an art.' Originally from 'The Soul of Whitney' (by Joy Duckett Cain), *Essence*, December 1990; cited from Classic Whitney, www.classicwhitney.com/interview/essence_1990.htm

Houston, Whitney – 'My daughter is my greatest inspiration.' Originally from an interview on *Access Hollywood*; cited from 'Whitney Houston's Final Interview: Singer Said She Had "Matured"' (by Radar Staff), RadarOnline.com, February 2012, www.radaronline.com/exclusives/2012/02/whitney-houston-dead-final-interview-access-hollywood-video

Houston, Whitney – Their 'drug of choice' was weed laced with rock cocaine. She said that by the time she made *The Preacher's Wife*, she was using drugs everyday 'trying to hide pain'. She acknowledged that she was so in love with Bobby that 'he was [her] drug'. 'Whitney Houston Tells All', *The Oprah Winfrey Show*, Harpo Productions, HBO Films, HD Vision Studios, High Noon Productions, September 2009, www.oprah.com/entertainment/oprahs-exclusive-interview-with-whitney-houston/all

Houston, Whitney – 'I am not a person who wants to die. I am a person who has life and wants to live.' 'Whitney Houston – ABC Primetime Special Edition with Diane Sawyer', December 2002, uploaded to YouTube by The Whitney Houston Platinum Club, September 2022, www.youtube.com/watch?v=4ybE1Zlf8mM

Rock Hudson

Briggle, Stockton – 'We all just stood there and tried to comprehend that such a thing could have happened… So, Rock's ashes went out to sea, surrounded by a huge rainbow. That was finally how he was put at peace.' *All That Heaven Allows: A Biography of Rock Hudson* (by Mark Griffin), HarperCollins, December 2018

Collart, Yanou – '[Rock] wanted a big party with mariachis and champagne.' 'Hudson Cremated' (by Carla Hall), *The Washington Post*, October 1985, www.washingtonpost.com/archive/lifestyle/1985/10/04/hudson-cremated/64e74e65-a8ad-4338-9d79-0b02e779805f

Day, Doris – 'I just loved working with him. We laughed and laughed.' 'A New Heyday' (by Susan King), *Los Angeles Times*, January 2012, www.latimes.com/archives/la-xpm-2012-jan-05-la-et-doris-day-films-20120105-story.html

Evans, Linda – 'I saw how hard he tried to protect me… [Hudson was a] delightful human being… funny and deep and kind and charming.' *Rock Hudson: All That Heaven Allowed* (directed by Stephen Kijak), HBO

Documentary Films, Altitude Film Entertainment in association with Berlanti Schechter Films and Dog Star Films, June 2023

Fairchild, Morgan – '[Rock Hudson] gave AIDS a face.' 'The Show Goes on in AIDS Battle', BBC News, November 2003, news.bbc.co.uk/1/hi/entertainment/3281609.stm

Hudson, Rock – 'Someone asked me once what my philosophy of life was, and I said some crazy thing. I should have said, "How the hell do I know?"' Rock Hudson Tribute, www.rockhudsontribute.com/quotes

Heath Ledger

Farrell, Colin – '[It] was never about filling Heath's shoes as much as seeing them across the finish line.' Originally from a statement on *Access Hollywood*; cited from 'Colin Farrell On "The Imaginarium of Doctor Parnassus": "Never About Filling Heath's Shoes"', NBC Connecticut, January 2010, www.nbcconnecticut.com/news/national-international/colin_farrell_on_the_imaginarium_of_doctor_parnassus_never_about_filling_heath_s_shoes_/1877259

Ledger, Heath – 'Life is so short. It's like we're already gone, really, in retrospect.' 'A Balanced Ledger' (by *New York Daily News* Staff), *New York Daily News*, June 2000, www.nydailynews.com/2000/06/26/a-balanced-ledger-whats-his-motivation-not-fame-says-the-patriots21-year-old-heartthrob

Ledger, Heath – '[Took] the blond out of [his] career.' 'Heath Ledger's Lonesome Trail: the *Rolling Stone* Interview' (by David Lipsky), *Rolling Stone*, March 2006, www.rollingstone.com/tv-movies/tv-movie-news/heath-ledgers-lonesome-trail-the-rolling-stone-interview-247198/3

Ledger, Heath – 'It's the most fun I've had playing a role.' 'The Making Of Heath Ledger's Joker' (by Dan Jolin), *Empire*, July 2012, www.empireonline.com/movies/features/heath-ledger-joker

Ledger, Heath – 'This is to remind me never to smoke weed again.' '(Untitled Heath Ledger Project)' (by Chris Norris), *New York*, February 2008, www.nymag.com/news/features/44217

Ledger, Heath – 'I'm born to be a father. And I've been looking forward to this all my life.' 'Remembering Heath Ledger' (by Prairie Miller), NewsBlaze, January 2008, www.newsblaze.com/entertainment/movie-reviews/remembering-heath-ledger_3761

Ledger was allegedly no stranger to drug use, apparently stating in a video that he used to smoke five joints of cannabis a day for twenty years. 'Video Shows Ledger at Hollywood Drug Party', ABC News, January 2008, www.abcnews.go.com/Entertainment/Oscars2008/story?id=4218070&page=1

Mendelsohn, Ben – '[Cowboys] are the very symbol of American masculinity. This is one of the biggest heartthrobs on Earth taking on that character. That's balls. And that's an artist.' *I Am Heath Ledger* (directed by Adrian Buitenhuis and Derik Murray), Network Entertainment, May 2017

Bruce Lee

Account of Bruce Lee's death. *Bruce Lee: A Life* (by Matthew Polly), Simon & Schuster UK, June 2019

Lee, Bruce – 'I am not afraid to die... I will have no regrets, I did what I wanted to do... You can't expect more from life.' *Be Water, My Friend: The True Teachings of Bruce Lee* (by Shannon Lee), Rider, October 2020

Lee, Bruce – 'Empty your mind. Be formless, shapeless, like water... Water can flow or it can crash. Be water, my friend.' Originally said on the TV show *Longstreet*, then repeated on *The Pierre Berton Show*, December 1971; cited from 'Bruce Lee: The Lost Interview | Pierre Berton Show 1971', uploaded to YouTube by Bruce Lee Mania, March 2025 www.youtube.com/watch?v=ER5Z_MyUkJQ

Lee, Linda – 'All these years later, people still wonder about how Bruce died. I prefer to remember how he lived.' *The Life and Tragic Death of Bruce Lee* (by Linda Lee), Star, February 1975

Norris, Chuck – 'Lee was lightning fast, very agile and incredibly strong for his size.' Originally from an article in *Black Belt*; cited from 'What Chuck Norris really thought about Bruce Lee' (by Calum Russell), *Far Out*, June 2022, www.faroutmagazine.co.uk/what-chuck-norris-thought-bruce-lee

Linda Lovelace

Lovelace, Linda – 'She did things to keep her man happy; I did things to keep my man from killing me.' / 'I live for sex... I'm what you might call an exhibitionist.' / 'I had been brutalized, raped and forced into every sexual situation imaginable.' / '[She] liked to go down by the ocean and

hold hands.' / 'I felt like garbage.' *Ordeal* (by Linda Lovelace and Mike McGrady), Citadel Press, December 2017

Lovelace, Linda – 'There was a gun to my head the entire time.' 'Crime Hunter: Porn Movie Deep Throat Triggered Mob Mayhem' (by Brad Hunter), *Toronto Sun*, June 2022, www.torontosun.com/news/world/crime-hunter-porn-movie-deep-throat-triggered-mob-mayhem

MacKinnon, Catharine A. – '[Linda was] sweet, strong, smart and real.' 'Will We See the Truth about Linda Lovelace?' (by Rhys Blakely), *The Times*, February 2012, www.thetimes.com/travel/destinations/north-america-travel/us-travel/california/will-we-see-the-truth-about-linda-lovelace-wcqz5tw6tkd

Marchiano, Dominic – 'I am proud of my mom and hope [the film] will create a new awareness on the subject matter. She was a survivor... and a wonderful person.' Originally from an article in *The Sun*; cited from 'Linda Lovelace's Son Praises Biopic', *Express*, August 2013, www.express.co.uk/celebrity-news/423268/Linda-Lovelace-s-son-praises-biopic

Steve McQueen

A friend of McQueen's – 'If Steve McQueen had been alive today, he would have punched you out. He punched out people like you.' 'Last Chance Surgery, Steve McQueen Dies in Juarez, Nov. 1980' (by Trish Long), *El Paso Times*, eu.elpasotimes.com/story/news/2020/11/04/steve-mcqueen-last-chance-surgery-dies-juarez-due-cancer/3751114001/#

Coleman, Cliff – 'He calmly got in her car and that was the last we saw of him for two days.' 'Happy Happy Birthday Baby! Steve McQueen (b. 3/24/30): Fifty Years of the King of Cool' (by Christopher Sandford), *Bright Lights Film Journal*, March 2022, www.brightlightsfilm.com/steve-mcqueen-fifty-years-of-the-king-of-cool

McQueen, Steve – 'I live for myself and I answer to nobody.' '14 Brilliant Life Lessons From Steve McQueen' (by Benjamin Cooper), Airows, October 2015, www.airows.com/culture/14-life-lessons-steve-mcqueen

McQueen, Steve – 'I'm not sure whether I'm an actor who races or a racer who acts.' 'The King of Cool – Steve McQueen' (by Jack Parrott), *Car & Classic*, February 2025, www.carandclassic.com/magazine/the-king-of-cool-steve-mcqueen

McQueen, Steve – 'I come from the gutter.' *Steve McQueen: The Man & Le Mans* (directed by Gabriel Clarke and John McKenna), Noah Media Group, Content Media, McQueen Racing, Pit Lane Productions, November 2015

McQueen, Steve – 'Mexico is showing the world a new way of fighting cancer through nonspecific metabolic therapies… Thank you for helping to save my life.' / With one doctor calling the therapy 'rank quackery'. 'McQueen's Legacy of Laetrile' (by Barron H. Lerner), *The New York Times*, November 2005, www.nytimes.com/2005/11/15/health/mcqueens-legacy-of-laetrile.html

McQueen said the United States Marine Corps 'made a man out of [him]'. *Steve McQueen: In His Own Words* (by Marshall Terrill), Dalton Watson Fine Books, June 2020

McQueen-Toffel, Neile – She recounts their rollercoaster fifteen-and-a-half-year marriage, revealing 'his good side, his crazy side, his dark side'. She wrote that his jealousy and paranoia once saw him beating her, and holding a gun to her head, demanding to know who she had had a fling with. *My Husband, My Friend* (by Neile McQueen-Toffel), AuthorHouse, November 2006

Santos Vargas, Dr Cesar – '[He was] a man sure of himself and very sincere… He had a desire to live when he knew the race [against death] was at a short distance.' 'Last Chance Surgery, Steve McQueen Dies in Juarez, Nov. 1980' (by Trish Long), *El Paso Times*, eu.elpasotimes.com/story/news/2020/11/04/steve-mcqueen-last-chance-surgery-dies-juarez-due-cancer/3751114001/#

Marilyn Monroe

Cukor, George – Described her death as 'a nasty business', saying, 'Her worst rejection. Power and money. In the end she was too innocent.' 'Marilyn Monroe's Final Hours: Nuke Fears, Mob Spies, and a Secret Kennedy Visitor' (by Anthony Summers), *Vanity Fair*, March 2022, www.vanityfair.com/hollywood/2022/03/marilyn-monroes-final-hours

DiMaggio, Joe (recounted by Engelberg, Morris) – 'I'll finally get to see Marilyn.' 'For Love of DiMaggio' (by Buzz Bissinger), *Vanity Fair*, September 2000, archive.vanityfair.com/article/2000/9/for-love-of-dimaggio

Fitzgerald, Ella – '[Marilyn was] an unusual woman – a little ahead of her times. And she didn't know it'. Originally from an article in *Ms.* magazine, August 1972; cited from 'Marilyn Monroe Helped Ella Fitzgerald Break a Racial Barrier With a Phone Call' (by Stefan Andrews), The Vintage News, December 2017, www.thevintagenews.com/2017/12/17/marilyn-monroe-ella-fitzgerald

Hefner, Hugh – 'Spending eternity next to Marilyn is too sweet to pass up.' 'For Sale: Eternity with Marilyn Monroe' (by Jeff Gottlieb), *Los Angeles Times*, August 2009, www.latimes.com/archives/la-xpm-2009-aug-14-me-marilyn14-story.html

Monroe, Marilyn – 'We should all start to live before we get too old. Fear is stupid. So are regrets.' Originally from an interview with W. J. Weatherby, 1960; cited from 'The Best Marilyn Monroe Quotes That Showed the Real Woman (Plus the Most Famous One She Never Said)', She Wore Stars, www.sheworestars.com/blog/marilyn-monroe-quotes

Monroe, Marilyn – 'It's not true I had nothing on, I had the radio on.' 'Cinema: Something for the Boys', *Time*, August 1952, www.time.com/archive/6794806/cinema-something-for-the-boys

Monroe, Marilyn – 'Will you say goodbye to Pat [Lawford's wife] and to Jack [the President] and to yourself, because you're a nice guy?' *The Fixer: Moguls, Mobsters, Movie Stars, and Marilyn* (by Josh Young and Manfred Westphal), Grand Central Publishing, May 2024

'No other star has ever inspired such a wide range of emotions – from lust to pity, from envy to remorse.' *The Guide to United States Popular Culture* (edited by Ray B. Browne and Pat Browne), Bowling Green University Popular Press, September 1990

'[She was a] shrewd businesswoman.' 'Cinema: Who Would Resist?', *Time*, August 1952, www.time.com/archive/6826720/cinema-who-would-resist

Wilder, Billy – 'For what you finally got on screen, she was worth every hour you had to wait for her… How often do you have a face like hers that lights up a screen?' *The Hollywood Book of Death* (by James Robert Parish), McGraw-Hill, October 2001

Brittany Murphy

Bertolotti, Angelo – 'I have a feeling that there was a definite murder situation here.' 'Brittany Murphy's Father Says She Was Poisoned', *Good*

Morning America, ABC News, November 2013, www.abcnews.go.com/GMA/video/brittany-murphy-poisoned-claims-actress-father-20934104

'Huggable, not fuckable.' Originally from an article in *Interview*, 2000; cited from *What Happened, Brittany Murphy?* (directed by Cynthia Hill), HBO, Blumhouse Television, Pyramid Productions, October 2021

Jordan, Trista – 'Simon had taken a red tube of lipstick and drawn lips outside her natural lip line like a clown. Her blush was lopsided.' *What Happened, Brittany Murphy?* (directed by Cynthia Hill), HBO, Blumhouse Television, Pyramid Productions, October 2021

Monjack, Simon – The 'closeness and beauty of [their] love will live on forever'. 'Brittany a "Bright Light that Lit the World"' (by Danielle Teutsch), *The Sydney Morning Herald*, December 2009, www.smh.com.au/entertainment/celebrity/brittany-a-bright-light-that-lit-the-world-20091226-lfnh.html

Murphy, Brittany – 'I would like to be very, very, very, very old. With all the technology we are inventing and what they are coming up with scientifically, people are having longer lifetimes.' Originally from an article in *Interview*, December/January 2003; cited from 'From the Vault: Brittany Murphy Opens up to Drew Barrymore', November 2021, www.interviewmagazine.com/film/from-the-vault-brittany-murphy-opens-up-to-drew-barrymore

Murphy, Brittany – 'I look at old photos of the premiere of *Clueless* and I look like a meatball on top of another meatball.' 'A Keen Sense of Selves' (by Quendrith Johnson), *Los Angeles Times*, September 2001, www.latimes.com/archives/la-xpm-2001-sep-09-ca-43649-story.html

Murphy, Brittany and Murphy, Sharon – 'We love Simon and we believe Simon.' *What Happened, Brittany Murphy?* (directed by Cynthia Hill), HBO, Blumhouse Television, Pyramid Productions, October 2021

Murphy, Sharon – 'The lab Angelo used, if you can call it that, is an internet site that farmed out the actual testing and then wrote horribly untrue things under the guise of "analysis".' She wrote that Angelo's accusations were self-serving and that he only wanted to trade on Brittany's life, career and good reputation 'at the cost of putting a cloud over her memory.' 'Brittany Murphy's Mother Breaks Silence, Disputes Poison Claim in Emotional Open Letter (Exclusive)' (by Sharon Murphy), *The Hollywood Reporter*, November 2013, www.hollywoodreporter.com/news/general-news/brittany-murphys-mother-breaks-silence-659529

Najimy, Kathy – Simon had come along during a time in Brittany's life when she was having 'a little dip' and she became 'prey'. *What Happened, Brittany Murphy?* (directed by Cynthia Hill), HBO, Blumhouse Television, Pyramid Productions, October 2021

Oakenfold, Paul – Described her as 'cool' and 'unique', with a strong, powerful voice. 'Her voice is great on the record, I think people will be surprised when they hear it.' 'Paul Oakenfold ft. Brittany Murphy – Faster Kill Pussycat – Behind the Scenes pt. 1', uploaded to YouTube by Paul Oakenfold, January 2009, www.youtube.com/watch?v=R8bDJ_AbfWo

Silverstone, Alicia – 'You guys! Did you see that?' 'Alicia Silverstone Remembers Being Stunned by Brittany Murphy's *Clueless* Audition' (by Christian Holub), *Entertainment Weekly*, February 2023, www.ew.com/movies/alicia-silverstone-remembers-brittany-murphy-clueless-audition

Stern, Howard – '[She was] the fat, ugly chick [from *Clueless*].' *The Howard Stern Show,* October 2003

Chris Penn

'An unfair end to a unique career… It was as if he were the Billy Carter of Hollywood – spending his life getting busted on Sunset Boulevard and bumming cash off his Oscar-winning brother.' 'Appreciation / Let Us Praise Chris Penn – in All His Guises' (by Peter Hartlaub), SFGate, January 2006, www.sfgate.com/entertainment/article/appreciation-let-us-praise-chris-penn-in-all-2523552.php

'[Chris Penn was] a human hand grenade who lived to pull his own pin… He was a nasty daredevil, fearless and playful and game for anything.' 'It Hurts to Look: Christopher Penn, 1965 – 2006' (by Matt Zoller Seitz), *Slant*, January 2006, www.slantmagazine.com/film/it-hurts-to-look-christopher-penn-19652006

Madsen, Michael – Recalled one wild night when the pair broke into a bar/liquor store. He described his friend as a 'wonderful, wonderful guy' and a 'tough son of a gun.' / '[I] cried for days and days… They don't make people like that any more.' 'Michael Madsen and Chris Penn Broke Into a Liquor Store', Opie Radio, uploaded to YouTube May 2016, www.youtube.com/watch?v=HkRoG7Lpf9I

'One of Hollywood's most perplexing actors.' 'The Price of Fame: the Final Reel of Chris Penn' (by Andrew Gumbel), *The Independent*, January 2006, www.independent.co.uk/news/world/americas/the-price-of-fame-the-final-reel-of-chris-penn-524557.html

Penn, Chris – 'More power to the people who get to choose their roles. I don't.' 'Chris Penn: Quotes', IMDb, www.imdb.com/name/nm0001606/quotes

Penn, Chris – 'Everybody says "Chris, you're a great character actor". I mean, my whole career. Why? Because I'm fat?... How about just I'm a good actor?' 'Chris Penn's Death – BLVD of Broken Dreams from E!', uploaded to YouTube by TheMediaDirectory, March 2018, www.youtube.com/watch?v=t_AajyzBHPg

Penn, Chris – 'When I act, I don't even know there's a camera there, don't care.' 'An Interview in the Back of a Truck with Chris Penn' as part of *Reservoir Dogs: Original Interviews*, Artisan Home Entertainment, August 2002

Penn, Sean – '[He has been] a fantastically self-abusing guy over periods of his life... It was a natural death. But a natural death that was brought on by some hard living, but particularly weight.' / Likened losing his brother to 'losing an arm'. *Larry King Live*, CNN, September 2006, transcripts.cnn.com/show/lkl/date/2006-09-14/segment/01

Matthew Perry

Crane, David – '[Helping other addicts] absolutely became his purpose, his reason for being.' '"Friends" Creator says She and Matthew Perry Discussed His Sobriety Journey at "Friends" Reunion' (by Drew Weisholtz), November 2023, *Today*, NBC, www.today.com/popculture/tv/friends-creators-discuss-matthew-perrys-sobriety-today-show-rcna123119

Friends, Lovers, and the Big Terrible Thing (by Matthew Perry), Headline (UK), Flatiron Books (USA), November 2022

Kauffman, Marta – Perry had wanted to 'help other addicts and it gave him purpose'. '"Friends" Creator says She and Matthew Perry Discussed His Sobriety Journey at "Friends" Reunion' (by Drew Weisholtz), November 2023, *Today*, NBC, www.today.com/popculture/tv/friends-creators-discuss-matthew-perrys-sobriety-today-show-rcna123119

Roberts, Julia – '[He is] awfully clever and funny and handsome.' *Late Show with David Letterman*, CBS, Worldwide Pants, February 1996

River Phoenix

'Clean life, dirty death.' 'Wasted', *The Canberra Times*, December 1993; cited from Trove, National Library of Australia, www.trove.nla.gov.au/newspaper/article/127253832/13975211

Feldman, Corey – 'Anybody that does enough drugs to OD is somebody that's a drug addict.' 'Wasted', *The Canberra Times*, December 1993; cited from Trove, National Library of Australia, www.trove.nla.gov.au/newspaper/article/127253832/13975211

Mathis, Samantha – She remembered him as 'sensitive and obsessive' and said that 'he felt things on his heart very deeply.' / 'I think he'd be acting, directing, saving the environment, just living and hanging out. Oh gosh, wouldn't that be nice?' 'The Untold Story of Lost Star River Phoenix – 25 Years After His Death' (by Hadley Freeman), *The Guardian*, October 2018, www.theguardian.com/film/2018/oct/25/the-untold-story-of-lost-star-river-phoenix-25-years-after-his-death

Phoenix, Arlyn/Heart – 'River was not a regular drug user… the excitement and energy of the Halloween nightclub and party scene were way beyond his usual experience and control. How many other beautiful young souls… have died using drugs recreationally?' 'A Mother's Note on Her Son's Life and Death', *Los Angeles Times*, November 1993, www.latimes.com/archives/la-xpm-1993-11-24-ca-60381-story.html

Phoenix, Joaquin – 'It was a complete and total joke. It was just fucking with the press… because he was so tired of being asked ridiculous questions.' '"I Fucking Love My Life": Joaquin Phoenix on Joker, Why River Is His Rosebud, His Rooney Research, and His "Prenatal" Gift for Dark Characters' (by Joe Hagan), *Vanity Fair*, November 2019, www.vanityfair.com/hollywood/2019/10/joaquin-phoenix-cover-story

Phoenix, River – 'I'd rather quit while I was ahead. There's no need in overstaying your welcome.' 'River Phoenix *E!* Interview, 1988', uploaded to YouTube by rivjudephoenix, May 2019, www.youtube.com/watch?v=MS-ZuGVS2GE

Phoenix, River – '[I] wouldn't eat a hamburger for $40,000.' 'Celebrating the Life of Cult Actor River Phoenix' (by Tish Wrigley and Ben Cobb), *AnOther*, November 2013, www.anothermag.com/another-man/3164/celebrating-the-life-of-cult-actor-river-phoenix

Phoenix, River – 'You start disintegrating, and you can't see yourself, and you just feel like you're being absorbed into a big blob of glitter.' 'Let It Flow' (by Lisa Bernhard), *Rolling Stone*, October 1991; cited from Aleka.org, www.aleka.org/phoenix/zines/phoeni29.html

Phoenix, River – 'This guy is schizophrenic.' From an article in *Première* (by Jean-Paul Chaillet), October 1993

Reiner, Rob – 'When River came in to audition, it was obvious that he was just an amazing, amazing talent.' 'The Untold Story of Lost Star River Phoenix – 25 Years After His Death' (by Hadley Freeman), *The Guardian*, October 2018, www.theguardian.com/film/2018/oct/25/the-untold-story-of-lost-star-river-phoenix-25-years-after-his-death

'Vegan James Dean.' 'Where Were You When River Phoenix Died?: the Vegan James Dean is Being Mourned by Teenagers from Ilkley to Bristol, Says Rose Rouse' (by Rose Rouse), *The Independent*, November 1993, www.independent.co.uk/life-style/where-were-you-when-river-phoenix-died-the-vegan-james-dean-is-being-mourned-by-teenagers-from-ilkley-to-bristol-says-rose-rouse-1502720.html

Weir, Peter – 'He was obviously going to be a movie star... It's something apart from the acting ability. Laurence Olivier never had what River had.' 'Wasted: How on Earth Did River Phoenix, Purest of All Child Stars, Sensitive, Clean-Living and Eco-Friendly, End Up Dead from a Drug Overdose at the Age of 23? The Answer Lies in a Secret Life that Was Shocking Even by the Notorious Double Standards of Hollywood' (by Ian Parker), *The Independent*, December 1993, www.web.archive.org/web/20130719174348/https://www.independent.co.uk/arts-entertainment/wasted-how-on-earth-did-river-phoenix-purest-of-all-child-stars-sensitive-cleanliving-and-ecofriendly-end-up-dead-from-a-drug-overdose-at-the-age-of-23-the-answer-lies-in-a-secret-life-that-was-shocking-even-by-the-notorious-double-standards-of-hollywood-1465475.html

Elvis Presley

Dylan, Bob – 'Hearing [Elvis] for the first time was like busting out of jail.' Originally from an article in *US Weekly*, August 1987; cited from 'Went to See the Gypsy', The Bob Dylan Commentaries, www.bobdylancommentaries.com/went-to-see-the-gypsy

Hanks, Tom – 'Look, Elvis was Picasso. He was a one-of-a-kind, once-in-a-lifetime artist.' 'Baz Luhrmann is Ready for Rhinestones, Cadillacs, Dr. Feelgood and a Svengali' (by Maureen Dowd), *The New York Times*, May 2022, www.nytimes.com/2022/05/21/style/baz-luhrmann-elvis.html

Lipton, Peggy – Elvis 'kissed like a god'. *Breathing Out* (by Peggy Lipton with David and Coco Dalton), St Martin's Press, June 2005

Presley, Elvis – 'Every time I think that I'm getting old, and gradually going to the grave, something else happens.' '20 Memorable Elvis Presley Quotes' (by Jennifer M. Wood), Mental Floss, January 2020, www.mentalfloss.com/article/90653/20-memorable-elvis-presley-quotes

Rodgers, Garry – Would have chalked up Elvis's death to 'cardiac arrhythmia antecedent to hypertensive cardiovascular disease with atherosclerotic heart disease antecedent to polypharmacy antecedent to autoimmune inflammatory disorder antecedent to traumatic brain injury'. 'Elvis Presley's Death – What Really Killed the King?' (by Garry Rodgers), February 2016, *HuffPost*, www.huffpost.com/entry/elvis-presleys-death-what_b_9157820

Wallis, Hal – 'A Presley picture is the only sure thing in Hollywood.' 'Quotes About Elvis', Graceland, www.graceland.com/quotes-about-elvis

Kelly Preston

Preston, Kelly – 'I would like to end world hunger and create world peace.' / 'Keeping it all normal and keeping us together is my first priority. Then I fit films into my life.' 'Sky High (2005) – Q&A Interview with Kelly Preston' (by Elaine Lipworth), Phase9, October 2005, www.phase9.tv/movies-and-tv/sky-high-2005-q-and-a-interview-with-kelly-preston.shtml

Preston, Kelly – '[We dance] all the time… I love it.' 'Love At First Sight For Kelly Preston And John Travolta? | WWHL', Watch What Happens Live with Andy Cohen, June 2018, www.youtube.com/watch?v=0mMD0hDaQ-0

Travolta, Ella Bleu – Talked of how 'fun and exciting and wonderful' her mum made every situation, every holiday, every birthday. 'Every activity was so heightened because of the life she put into it.' 'John Travolta's Daughter Ella Travolta On Working w/ Dad & Song Honoring Late Mom', *Access Hollywood*, September 2024, www.youtube.com/watch?v=ufY_qvYIoEQ

Christopher Reeve

Hepburn, Katharine – 'You're going to be a big star, Christopher, and support me in my old age.' *Still Me* (by Christopher Reeve), Penguin Random House, 1999

Mouthed to his wife Dana, 'Maybe we should let me go.' She tearfully responded that she would support whatever decision he made, adding, 'You're still you.' / 'You play the hand you're dealt. I think the game's worthwhile.' *Super/Man: The Christopher Reeve Story* (directed by Ian Bonhôte and Peter Ettedgui), DC Studios, Passion Pictures, Misfits Entertainment and Jenco Films, in association with HBO Documentary Films, CNN Films and Words + Pictures, November 2024

'One of the brightest, informed, alert, sensitive and caring men [sic]... who smiled quickly, easily and frequently.' 'Christopher Reeve: A Life for All Seasons – October 31, 2004' (by Reverend Frank Hall), The Unitarian Universalist Congregation in Westport, uploaded September 2010, www.uuwestport.org/christopher-reeve-a-life-for-all-seasons-october-31-2004

Reeve, Christopher – 'You can see how easily it can happen. One moment everything is fine and then the world falls apart.' Originally from a TV interview; cited from 'Christopher Reeve: Living in Hope' (by Andrew Walker), BBC News, news.bbc.co.uk/1/hi/in_depth/uk/2000/newsmakers/1849218.stm

Wayne, John – 'This is our new man. He's taking over.' 'The Actor John Wayne Thought Would Succeed Him: "He's Taking Over"' (by Michael Gordon), *Far Out*, August 2025, www.faroutmagazine.co.uk/actor-john-wayne-thought-would-succeed-him-hes-taking-over

Patrick Swayze

***City of Joy* described as 'well-intentioned but mostly bland'.** Review in *Kalamazoo Gazette* (by James Sanford), July 2002

'Doesn't want to be the poster boy for living with cancer.' / 'When it looks like I may live longer than five minutes, I'll drop cigarettes like a hot potato.' *Barbara Walters Special – Patrick Swayze: The Truth,* ABC News, January 2009

Grey, Jennifer – 'When I think of him, I think of being in his arms when we were kids, dancing, practicing the lift in the freezing lake, having a blast doing this tiny little movie we thought no one would ever see.' 'Stars Pay

Tribute to Patrick Swayze, the Brave Cowboy and Star of *Dirty Dancing*' (by Alun Palmer), *The Mirror*, September 2009, www.mirror.co.uk/3am/celebrity-news/stars-pay-tribute-to-patrick-swayze-418894

Hygate, Rosemary – '[He] was passionate and intense about everything. Everything.' *I Am Patrick Swayze* (directed by Adrian Buitenhuis), Network Entertainment, Paramount Network, August 2019

'Macho guy with the soul of a poet.' *I Am Patrick Swayze* (directed by Adrian Buitenhuis), Network Entertainment, Paramount Network, August 2019

Moore, Demi – '[He had] a beautiful balance between strength and softness.' *I Am Patrick Swayze* (directed by Adrian Buitenhuis), Network Entertainment, Paramount Network, August 2019

Petty, Lori – 'An open book.' *I Am Patrick Swayze* (directed by Adrian Buitenhuis), Network Entertainment, Paramount Network, August 2019

Swayze, Don – 'Without putting down his books or violin, he did a little sweep with his legs and took both of them out. I grew up with a superhero in my family.' *I Am Patrick Swayze* (directed by Adrian Buitenhuis), Network Entertainment, Paramount Network, August 2019

Swayze, Patrick – 'The longer your life goes on, the more death you face.' 'Drink, Suicide and Why I Turned Against Hollywood' (by Lester Middlehurst), *Daily Mail*, November 2005, www.dailymail.co.uk/tvshowbiz/article-370048/Drink-suicide-I-turned-Hollywood

Swayze, Patrick – Admitted he was a 'not-very-pretty drunk'. From an article in *Playboy*, June 1992

Swayze, Patrick – 'It's like kids are the one thing that's missing at the ranch.' *The Time of My Life* (by Patrick Swayze and Lisa Niemi), Simon & Schuster, October 2009

Swayze, Patrick – He declared that he refused to 'chase staying alive', instead opting to 'live'. *Barbara Walters Special – Patrick Swayze: The Truth,* ABC News, January 2009

Sharon Tate

Atkins, Susan – Recalling that Tex had announced: 'I'm the devil and I'm here to do the devil's business.' 'Susan Atkins Interview (1976) – Description of Sharon Tate Murder (Manson Murder)', uploaded to YouTube by elizabeth orr, January 2013, www.youtube.com/watch?v=0q-LiARYmqc

Duke, Patty – Called her 'a gentle, gentle creature', adding, 'I was crazy about her, and I didn't know anyone who wasn't'. 'Sharon Tate' (by Anne Dingus), *Texas Monthly*, August 1999, www.texasmonthly.com/articles/sharon-tate

Farrow, Mia – '[She was] as sweet and pure a human being as I have ever known.' 'From Beauty to Tragedy: Candid and Beautiful Photos of Sharon Tate during the 1960s', Rare Historical Photos, www.rarehistoricalphotos.com/sharon-tate-old-photos

King, Greg – 'Sharon's real legacy lies not in her movies… The very fact that victims or their families in California are able to sit before those convicted of a crime and have a voice in the sentencing at trials… is largely due to the work of Doris [and Patti] Tate.' *Sharon Tate and the Manson Murders* (by Greg King), Barricade Books, May 2000

Polanski, Roman – 'Even after so many years, I find myself unable to watch a spectacular sunset or visit a lovely old house… without instinctively telling myself how much she would have loved it all. In these ways I shall remain faithful to her till the day I die.' *Sharon Tate: Recollection* (by Debra Tate), Running Press, June 2014

Reviewers describing her as 'frisky and cute' and 'delicious in her role as the antique dealer'. '*Twelve Plus One*: User Reviews', IMDb, July 2002 and October 2009, www.imdb.com/title/tt0065361/reviews

Robson, Mark – 'That's a great girl you're living with. Few actresses have her kind of vulnerability. She's got a great future.' *Roman by Polanski* (by Roman Polanski), William Heinemann, January 1984

'Sharon Tate is one of the most smashing young things to hit Hollywood in a long time.' 'The New American Beauties', *Newsweek*, March 1968, www.web.archive.org/web/20091024073308/http://geocities.com/cean2/newsweek.htm

Tarantino, Quentin – Described her as 'almost too good to be true' and a 'really nifty person', adding, 'I think it's horrible that she's been defined by her murder'. 'Quentin Tarantino Shares Why He Had to Tell Sharon Tate's Story', *The Jess Cagle Show* for Sirius XM, July 2021, www.youtube.com/watch?v=_OqPp5lJ0l0

Tate, Sharon – 'My whole life has been decided by fate.' From an interview with Enrico di Pompeo, July 1969

Tate, Sharon – 'I honestly don't understand the big fuss made over nudity and sex in films. It's silly.' / 'It's a terrible movie... Sometimes I say things I shouldn't. I guess I'm too outspoken.' *Sharon Tate and the Manson Murders* (by Greg King), Barricade Books, May, 2000

Tate, Sharon – 'We have a good arrangement. Roman lies to me and I pretend to believe him.' 'Sufferings of the Great Seducer' (by Peter Evans), *The Times*, July 2005, www.thetimes.com/best-law-firms/profile-legal/article/sufferings-of-the-great-seducer-2gtg9zrrgpv

Tate, Sharon – 'I don't fool myself – I can't see myself doing Shakespeare.' *All Eyes on Sharon Tate*, Metro-Goldwyn-Mayer, 1966

'The imperfect couple... Cool, nomadic, talented and nicely shocking.' Sufferings of the Great Seducer' (by Peter Evans), *The Times*, July 2005, www.thetimes.com/best-law-firms/profile-legal/article/sufferings-of-the-great-seducer-2gtg9zrrgpv

Paul Walker

DeGeneres, Ellen – 'When we book you, we have to add three extra minutes for screaming because it happens every time you come on.' *The Ellen DeGeneres Show*, A Very Good Production Inc., Telepictures Productions, Time Telepictures Television, WAD Productions, October 2005

Gibson, Tyrese – 'Some dudes, where they're handsome and they become arrogant with it and they're unapproachable... He wasn't intimidating because he was so regular and so grounded and so cool.' *I Am Paul Walker* (directed by Adrian Buitenhuis), Network Entertainment, Paramount Network, August 2018

Gibson, Tyrese – 'Paul lived in Santa Barbara. When something happened in the Philippines, he jumps off of his surfboard... and he's on a plane to the other side of the world, to do any means necessary to make a difference.' 'Paul Walker Tribute The Noble Awards 2015 (Official/Original)', uploaded to YouTube by Noble Awards, April 2015, www.youtube.com/watch?v=tMTZcnrat90

Rodriguez, Michelle – '[He] just *loves.*' / '[His heart was] so open and full of wanting to give.' 'Paul Walker Tribute The Noble Awards 2015 (Official/

Original)', uploaded to YouTube by Noble Awards, April 2015, www.youtube.com/watch?v=tMTZcnrat90

Walker, Meadow – The foundation aims to simply 'do good' by fulfilling Paul's legacy via 'his passion for the ocean, his passion for rescuing animals, his passion for helping people and his passion for spontaneous goodwill.' Posted on Instagram by meadowwalker, September 2015, www.instagram.com/p/7iVaRXNB-D/?hl=en-gb

Walker's mother described Vin Diesel as her son's 'other half'. Originally from a post on Facebook by Vin Diesel; cited from 'Paul Walker: Vin Diesel's Tribute To "Brother"', Sky News, December 2013, news.sky.com/story/paul-walker-vin-diesels-tribute-to-brother-10425403

Walker, Paul – 'The dream is to have it all... You only live one time – I want to get it all in.' 'Paul Walker Shares His Dream in Last *ET* Interview' (by Robert Pace), Entertainment Tonight, December 2013, www.etonline.com/news/141304_Paul_Walker_Last_Interview

Walker, Paul – 'Would that be so bad?' 'Paul Walker on Parkour, Stalkers and Sharks' (by Nick Carvell), *GQ*, December 2013, www.gq-magazine.co.uk/article/paul-walker-interview-for-davidoff-cool-water

Walker, Paul – 'I'm a doer, and whether it was the tsunami in Sri Lanka or the earthquake in Indonesia, I was always saying, "I should be there; I should be helping out".' 'Find Your Balance' (by Nino Munoz and Dan Jones), *Men's Health*, January 2010, www.menshealth.com/trending-news/a19524544/life-and-success-tips-paul-walker

Walker, Paul – '[I was probably] the illegal U-turn king of LA.' 'Paul Walker Kicks into High Gear' (by Louis B. Hobson), Jam! Showbiz, June 2001, www.archive.vn/20130922000611/http://jam.canoe.ca/Movies/Artists/W/Walker_Paul/2001/06/17/762482.html#selection-773.1-773.36

Robin Williams

Crystal, Billy – 'For almost forty years, he was the brightest star in a comedy galaxy.' 'Watch Billy Crystal's Touching Tribute to Robin Williams at the Emmys' (by Aisha Harris), *Slate*, August 2014, www.slate.com/culture/2014/08/billy-crystal-honors-robin-williams-at-the-2014-emmys-video.html

Gillian, Terry – Said that the actor had the ability to 'go from manic to mad to tender and vulnerable' and that he had 'the most unique mind on the planet'. Originally from an article in *Playboy* (by Lawrence Grobel), January 1992; cited from 'The 1992 Playboy Interview With Robin Williams', October 2024, www.playboy.com/read/the-1992-playboy-interview-with-robin-williams

Levy, Shawn – 'It was clear to all of us on that set that something was going on with Robin.' *Robin's Wish* (directed by Tylor Norwood), Quotable Pictures, 2020

Miller, Bruce – 'People who are incredibly brilliant can tolerate degenerative diseases better. Robin Williams was a genius.' *Robin's Wish* (directed by Tylor Norwood), Quotable Pictures, 2020

Obama, Barack – 'Robin Williams was an airman, a doctor, a genie, a nanny, a president, a professor, a bangarang, Peter Pan, and everything in between… He arrived in our lives as an alien – but he ended up touching every element of the human spirit.' 'Statement by the President on the Passing of Robin Williams', The White House, August 2014, obamawhitehouse.archives.gov/the-press-office/2014/08/11/statement-president-passing-robin-williams

Schneider Williams, Susan – 'Robin was losing his mind and he was aware of it.' / It was devastating to see 'the bravest man in the world playing the hardest role of his life'. 'The Terrorist Inside My Husband's Brain' (by Susan Schneider Williams), *Neurology*, September 2016, www.neurology.org/doi/full/10.1212/WNL.0000000000003162

Smith, Will – 'Our family is being honored from one Genie family to another.' Posted on Instagram by willsmith, October 2020, www.instagram.com/p/CF-mYTUBgS/

Williams, Robin – 'Death is nature's way of saying, "Your table is ready".' *The Fourth – And By Far the Most Recent – 637 Best Things Anybody Has Ever Said* (by Robert Byrne), Atheneum, September 1990

Williams, Robin – 'Self goes away. Ego, bye-bye. The thing that matters is others. That's what life's about.' From an interview with Diane Sawyer on *Good Morning America*, ABC News, October 2006

Natalie Wood

Account of the demise of Wagner and Wood's first marriage. *Natalie Wood: The Complete Biography* (by Suzanne Finstad), Crown Publishing Group, 2020

Dennis Davern's account of the night Natalie Wood died. *48 hours, Natalie Wood: Death in Dark Water* (directed by Matthew DeVoe), CBS Broadcasting, CBS News, February 2018

Gregson Wagner, Natasha – '[She took] enough sleeping pills to kill herself.' *Natalie Wood: What Remains Behind* (directed by Laurent Bouzereau), Amblin Television, HBO Documentary Films, Nedland Media, July 2020

Gregson Wagner, Natasha – 'My mom loved gardenias, so whenever I smell them, I always think of my mom.' 'How Natalie Wood's Daughter is Keeping Her Mother's Legacy Alive' (by Stephanie Saltzman), *Town & Country*, June 2016, www.townandcountrymag.com/style/beauty-products/news/a6480/natalie-wood-fragrance-natasha-gregson-wagner

Hernandez, Ralph – 'We have not been able to prove that this was a homicide, and we have not been able to prove that this was an accident, either. The ultimate problem is, we don't know how she ended up in the water.' *48 hours, Natalie Wood: Death in Dark Water* (directed by Matthew DeVoe), CBS Broadcasting, CBS News, February 2018

'Most exciting juvenile motion picture star of the year.' From an article in *Parents*, 1947

'Our sexual conscience on the silver screen.' 'Natalie Wood: Our Sexual Conscience on the Silver Screen', *L'Officiel/USA,* August 1980

Pollack, Sydney – 'When she was right for the part, there was no one better. She was a damn good actress.' 'It's Been 39 Years Since Natalie Wood "Drowned". Her Death is Still Shrouded in Mystery' (by Gemma Bath), Mamamia, May 2020, www.mamamia.com.au/natalie-wood-documentary

She had a 'dark fresh loveliness.' 'Natalie Wood: Portraits of a Legend' (by Ben Cosgrove), *Life*, December 1963, www.life.com/people/natalie-wood-rare-and-classic-photos-of-a-hollywood-legend

She was allegedly sexually assaulted by Hollywood star Kirk Douglas. *Little Sister* (by Lana Wood), Dey Street Books, November 2021

Welles, Orson – '[She was] so good, she was terrifying.' 'TV Weekend; A Documentary Remembrance of Natalie Wood' (by John J. O'Connor), *The New York Times*, July 1988, www.nytimes.com/1988/07/08/arts/tv-weekend-a-documentary-remembrance-of-natalie-wood.html

Wood, Lana (recounting what Natalie Wood had said) – 'Sometimes it's better to be with the devil you know than the devil you don't.' *48 hours, Natalie Wood: Death in Dark Water* (directed by Matthew DeVoe), CBS Broadcasting, CBS News, February 2018

Wood, Natalie – 'I'm just going to have to grow old because I'm too terrified to have anything done.' 'The Best 20 Natalie Wood Quotes', Medium, June 2022, quotesandsayings.medium.com/the-best-20-natalie-wood-quotes-90f48f69e5b3

Wood, Natalie – 'I really did think that Edmund Gwenn was Santa.' *Natasha: The Biography of Natalie Wood* (by Suzanne Finstad), Arrow, July 2002

Wood, Natalie – 'I've always been terrified of water, dark water, sea water.' Originally from an interview in the 1970s; cited from 'Inside Natalie Wood and Robert Wagner's Tumultuous, Ultimately Tragic Romance' (by Natalie Finn), E! News, February 2018, www.eonline.com/news/911264/inside-natalie-wood-and-robert-wagner-s-tumultuous-ultimately-tragic-romance?utm_source=eonline&utm_medium=rssfeeds&utm_campaign=imdb_topstories